The Art of Japanese
Swordsmanship

居合道

英信流

The Art of Japanese Swordsmanship

A Manual of Eishin-Ryu Iaido

居合道

by Nicklaus Suino

Weatherhill

New York & Tokyo

Warning: The techniques described in this book, and the techniques of any martial art, are dangerous if not practiced correctly. Neither the author nor the publishers of this book are responsible for the results of your choice to practice these techniques. You do so at your own risk. Please use caution when handling any weapons, and be sure to consult a qualified teacher before attempting to perform any new martial arts skills.

First edition, 1994
Fourth printing, 1998

Published by Weatherhill, Inc., of New York and Tokyo, with editorial offices at 568 Broadway, Suite 705, New York, N.Y. 10012

© 1994 by Nicklaus Suino. Protected by copyright under the terms of the International Copyright Union; all rights reserved.

Printed in the U.S.A.

Library of Congress Cataloging in Publication Data

Suino, Nicklaus
    Eishin-Ryu iaido: manual of traditional Japanese swordsmanship / by Nicklaus Suino.
        p.   cm.
    Includes bibliographical references and index.
    ISBN 0-8348-0300-3
    1. Iaido.   I. Title.   II. Title: Manual of Traditional Swordsmanship.
    GV1150.2.S85   1994
    796.8'6--dc20   93-40459
                                                          CIP

Contents

Preface   *vii*
Acknowledgments   *viii*
How to Use This Book   *ix*

Introduction   1
What is Iaido?   3
Why Practice Iaido?   6
A Brief History of Japanese Swordsmanship   8
The Evolution of Eishin-Ryu Iaido   12
What You Need to Practice Iaido   14
About the Japanese Sword   16
How to Wear the Obi and Hakama   20
Etiquette and the Code of the Samurai   23

Basic Techniques   25
How to Bow   27
Fundamentals of Practice   36
How to Read the Illustrations   42
Seated Set   43
Drawing Methods Set   83

The Intermediate and Advanced Practitioner   101
Intermediate and Advanced Practice   103
The Samurai Sitting Method   106
Eye Contact, Focus, and Dignity   108

Intermediate Techniques   111
Secret Forms, Drawing Methods Set   113
Half-Seated Set   126
Secret Forms, Standing Set   156

Advanced Techniques 187
    Secret Forms, Seated Set 189
    Secret Forms, Extra Set 209
    Sword Methods 222

Glossary 237
Bibliography 245
Index 247

Preface

I aido is a method of wielding the sword, one of the *budo* (martial arts) forms of the Japanese people, which has been passed down from ancient times and which has survived until the present day. The *i* in iaido refers both to the existence of body and that of spirit, and the *ai* refers to adaptability, the impromtu execution of movements whenever and wherever a correct response is called for. With these aspects in mind, I believe that iaido, as one of today's budo forms, provides an excellent means of healthy training for both the mind and the body.

Nicklaus Suino, the author of this book, is a devoted swordsman. He spent nearly five years in Japan, training at my dojo, in both basic and advanced techniques, and so developed his skills that the Muso Jikiden Eishin-Ryu Traditions Association awarded him his Sixth Dan certificate. Further, at events sponsored by the All Japan Iaido Federation, he won forms competitions up to the Fourth Dan level in the Kanto Region, and placed second among the best swordsmen in the nation at the Third Dan level. This sort of achievement is extremely rare, even among the Japanese.

I don't believe that there is any systematically written reference book such as this one for people who want to study iaido in North America. Both beginners and advanced students can use it for their reference. I'm sure anyone who shares our passion for Iaido will read it with pleasure.

Katsuo Yamaguchi
Hanshi Ninth Dan, Muso Jikiden Eishin Ryu Iaido
Hanshi, Eighth Dan, Kendo

範士九段山口克夫

Acknowledgments

No career in the martial arts is possible without teachers, and I have been very lucky in meeting a few exceptional teachers. The person most directly responsible for making it possible to write this book is Yamaguchi Katsuo Sensei, iaido teacher of Tokyo, Japan. His unwavering severity in practice has been matched only by the kindnesses shown to me by him and his wife when I visited their home. Though I can never repay him, this book is a small attempt to express my gratitude for everything he taught me. I have done my best to reproduce the techniques and ethics as he practices them. Any mistakes in this volume, however, are my own.

Sato Shizuya Sensei, Chief Director of Kokusai Budoin, IMAF (International Martial Arts Federation), provided the introduction to Yamaguchi Sensei and daily inspiration through his efforts to propagate traditional Japanese martial arts. Sensei Walter E. Todd of Oakland, California, wrote the introduction letter I needed to begin training with Sato Sensei and has provided countless insights into budo methods over the years.

Karl W. Scott III, Director of the Asian Martial Arts Studio in Ann Arbor, Michigan, is my original teacher of real budo and is one of the very few such men on the planet. I owe almost my entire martial arts career to his efforts.

Without John Gage, my training partner of over ten years, life in Japan would have been much lazier, and not nearly so rewarding, and without the support and encouragement of my wife, Suzanne, a life in the martial arts would be a very lonely one, indeed. This book is dedicated to these six people.

How to Use This Book

It is very difficult to learn martial arts from a book. In spite of this fact, there are hundreds of books on the martial arts—a few good ones—and there are perhaps ten books in English on Japanese swordsmanship of one kind or another. The shortcomings of books as martial arts teachers are many: a book can show pictures of techniques but it cannot show the motions between the checkpoints; a book cannot give you feedback about how well or poorly you are doing the technique; a book cannot remind you every day that you should follow the precepts of budo (unless you read it every day); and only a great book can give you an idea of the demeanor and presence of a great martial arts teacher. So why are all these books being written?

There are a few things a book can do. It can show you the checkpoints at various places in a form. This sort of knowledge is very valuable if you've ever studied with a teacher and want to refresh your memory. It can give you historical or cultural background information about the martial art you are studying. It can describe the correct attitude in practice and concepts you should strive to understand if you want to have a legitimate understanding of traditional Japanese martial culture. It can lead you to other sources of information.

I began writing this book with the intention of creating a reference manual of techniques for people who are studying Eishin-Ryu Iaido. Just before I returned to the United States, from Japan, my teacher said to me, "I want you to take responsibility for developing the art of iaido in America." Of course I had no idea of the work this would involve but, even if I had, I would have agreed to try. I have devoted myself to the study of this martial art, and part of the value system that accompanies training in any traditional martial art is duty to one's teacher. This book is one manifestation of that duty.

The concept of duty is one of the most misunderstood areas in budo, in my opinion. Students in the United States don't seem to realize that budo training has historically been a form of service. In China, the source of many forms of martial art, boxers served as guides and guardians for high-ranking persons. In Japan, the concept was raised to a higher level by the code of *bushido*, the way of the warrior, which made it clear that there was no greater glory than to die in service to one's lord. It may be easier to understand the modern equivalent of this by thinking of military service. The military exists to protect and serve its national government which, in this country at least, was created by and for the people. A person may advance his own aims while in military service, but the ultimate purpose of his existence as a soldier is to take the risk in war so that civilians do not have to. The general concept is learning to value some cause or purpose more than you value yourself. In matters of character, self-interest should diminish, service should improve. Yamamoto Tsunenori, in his book *Hagakure*, a manual of ethics for the samurai, expounds on this idea:

> *Some men are prone to having sudden inspirations. Some men do not quickly have good ideas but arrive at the answer by slow consideration. Well, if we investigate the heart of the matter, even though people's natural abilities differ . . . when your thinking rises above concern for your own welfare, wisdom which is independent of thought appears. Whoever thinks deeply on things, even though he may carefully consider the future, will usually think around the basis of his own welfare. By the result of such evil thinking he will only perform evil acts. It is very difficult for most silly fellows to rise above thinking of their own welfare.*

The martial artist exists to serve: his superiors; his city; his nation; the cause of greater good in the world. Somehow, the vast majority of martial arts practitioners in the United States have forgotten this, or have never been correctly taught in the first place, and are rightly thought of as ruffians.

One thing this book can do is educate you about a few of the cultural and philosophical aspects of budo training. Even at that, it probably won't have much effect. What you really need is a good teacher, and you need to spend enough time with him or her for the ethics and outlook that he or she has internalized to sink into your character. This may be more important than learning the techniques of your art, because a student with the right attitude can learn any technique, whereas techniques done with the wrong spirit can never purify the heart.

The value that techniques have is that they are an expression of how well you understand the principles of your martial art, and are also a means of affecting the spirit. That is why the majority of space in this book is devoted to explanations of techniques. You can find more information about history and sword making in other books but, as of this writing, there are no other books written in English that detail the techniques of Eishin-Ryu Iaido. The explanations offered here will help you practice correctly. The reason you must practice every day is to try to refine your techniques and, in so doing, refine your understanding of their underlying principles. This is part of what is meant by "character development." When you come to understand the relationship between the correct ethics, and outlook, of budo and the principles of the physical techniques, then your progress will speed forward.

It's hard work. Here is what you must do: find a good teacher, even if it is only at a seminar or camp. Practice what he or she teaches you every day, always trying to improve. Think about the purpose of the motions when you train, don't just run through them mechanically. When you aren't sure of a technique, consult this book to refresh your memory. Read the sections in this book about the special philosophical and cultural aspects of budo, and read as much about these subjects as you can in other books. Remember, great men devoted their lives to budo and did not become masters until they were very old. There's never enough time to practice, so you must devote yourself heart and soul to the time that you do spend. Be very critical of yourself. Always try to improve.

Introduction

What is Iaido?

*I*aido, *the way of the sword, is a martial art form that began as an off-shoot of* kenjutsu. *It was developed as a defensive method to counter surprise attacks and enemy raids in fifteenth and sixteenth century Japan.*

The purpose of iaido was to slay an opponent with one stroke of the sword immediately after unsheathing it. In order to create such a defense system, situations and circumstances of surprise attacks were studied to devise a systematized way to use the sword effectively against many forms of attack.

The practice of this martial art requires a solemn spirit, extreme concentration, and skill. Every motion, such as the movements of the arms or legs and body, must correspond to the offensive motions of the opponent, and it is of utmost importance that a person follow the rules of discipline that have been carefully and thoroughly applied.

The secret of iaido is a calm spirit. With a tranquil heart you put your hand on the hilt of your sword – in a split second your hand moves to cut down the opponent and resheath the sword – then return to your composed mind.

A serene spirit must be cultivated at all times. It is said that the sword is like the mind, and if the sword is upright, the mind is upright. But if the mind is not upright, the sword can never be wielded properly.

Even though you may devote yourself to it with all your heart and soul, it is very difficult to master iaido completely. It is possible, though, to move one step at a time toward the ultimate goal through practice. Many wise people have given their lives to iaido to make it what it is today. I believe that even though we live in a peaceful age, we have the responsibility and obligation to teach this part of our cultural heritage to the next generation.

Katsuo Yamaguchi
Tokyo, Japan

The physical practice of iaido includes drawing, parrying and cutting motions, as well as various methods for returning the sword to the scabbard. Most schools teach iaido using pre-arranged series of motions, sometimes called *kata*, or "forms." The motions are designed as defenses against attacks by an imaginary opponent, and each form teaches several principles of correct sword handling.

The art of iaido is a traditional art. Its forms are hundreds of years old, having been passed down from instructor to student since their creation. The teaching and practice methods are kept standardized by administration of the All Japan Iaido Federation in Japan, and by students of the art in other countries. Iaido is also traditional in the sense that it has no modern applications. Since there is no practical purpose for sword fighting methods in modern times, there is no reason to "update" the forms, or to make the art more effective for self-defense. Outside of physical fitness reasons and its historic value, therefore, iaido is mainly practiced as a means of character development.

There are other Japanese sword arts which differ slightly from iaido. Though every form includes blocking and cutting motions, everything that happens after the sword is outside the scabbard is more accurately called *kendo*. Kendo is practiced as a sport in Japan. *Kendoka* wear light body-armor, head protection and padded gloves, and score points by striking their opponents' vital areas with a bamboo stick, called a *shinai*. Both men and women practice kendo, often competing against each other. Since skill is much more important than size and strength, men have no special advantage.

Another Japanese sword art is called *batto-jutsu*. Batto-jutsu simply means "sword-drawing art." Most iaido schools practice only forms, but batto schools also practice cutting. They would soon run out of training partners if they cut one another, of course, so they use rolled straw mats, which have been soaked in water. The soaked mats are meant to provide a lifelike resistance to the blade.

Why, in iaido, do we place so much emphasis on drawing the sword? This emphasis is one aspect that remains from the days when these techniques were used in armed combat. A fraction of a second, or a millimeter's difference in position, could make all the difference to the outcome of a match with swords. The swords were razor-sharp, so even being touched with a blade meant a likely death. Getting the sword out of the scabbard and into the correct position quickly was crucial. What we practice now is an art, not a fighting method, so we strive for correct form and efficiency rather than deadly speed and accuracy.

By continually refining our technique we can improve concentration, develop physical skills, and learn about another culture's historical martial art and training methods. Many practice iaido as a second martial art, to compliment the more physical practice style of karate, judo, or aikido. As a first martial art, it is well suited to those who want to avoid over-exerting themselves, as well as to those who are collectors or aficionados of the Japanese sword.

Why Practice Iaido?

居合道家

Although many of the reasons for practicing Iaido are similar to those for other budo forms, its unique features make it somewhat different from them. Like other martial arts, there are physical fitness benefits from training. For example, iaido builds strong legs, a strong torso and arms, and helps to increase stamina, though not quite in the same way more energetic karate or judo training does. Iaido form practice is generally done at a slow, controlled pace. Iaido strengthens by long-term, careful repetition of precise motions, gradually refined over time, rather than by quick repetition or difficult calisthenics. The best *iaidoka* make the forms seem effortless, though any beginning student of the art will tell you how much effort is actually required.

The emphasis on control makes practice very safe (outside of the dangerous, live sword blade). Once the student learns a few basics of correct sword handling, there is almost no risk of injury. This is one reason that the art attracts many older people and people who have retired from other martial arts.

Another reason for controlled practice is improved concentration. By starting out with the large framework of the form and gradually adding details, the teacher helps the student master a spectrum of difficult skills. With time, the ability to concentrate improves, and students often find that their study or working habits become more efficient. Though this sort of benefit is common to all martial arts training, the particular type of training found in iaido seems to develop it especially well.

Traditional teachers of this sword art can give their students an authentic Japanese training experience. For American and European students, learning to do exactly as their teacher orders without asking a lot of questions can be a difficult task, but this is how it is done in Japan. There are several benefits to training without talking over every detail. Repeated practice can lead to a deep, intuitive understanding of the principles, unencumbered by the sort of intellectual analysis we Westerners tend toward. Students of Zen will recognize this feature from their experiences and, indeed, iaido is considered one of the better martial arts for conveying the concepts of Zen, along with kyudo, traditional Japanese archery.

The expression "acting without thinking" often has a negative connotation to us in the West but, seen in a different light, it can be a helpful motto for training. All the Japanese sword arts are descended from the feudal times of Japan, when men actually used swords to fight with and to defend themselves against their enemies. One concept which was often applied to training in those times was expressed in the phrase *muga mushin*. Roughly translated, this means "no self, no mind." The idea was that, if you trained hard enough for a long time and were able to put aside all thoughts of winning, the power of the gods (or what we might call "intuition" today) could act through your body and defeat your opponent. One major difficulty in achieving this state was that any sort of conceit would disrupt it. Just as the soldiers of feudal Japan were encouraged to put self-interest aside for the sake of their liege, today we strive to train without looking for short-term rewards or ego satisfaction. Instead, this long-term deepening of perception can lead to a serenity and clarity of outlook similar to that achieved by practioners of Zen, yoga and other meditation arts. Over time, iaidoka who train correctly come to have a greater ability to apprehend truth in the world around them: no small skill in this age of exaggeration and media hype, or in any age.

無我無心

A Brief History of Japanese Swordsmanship

居合道歴史

Japan is a unique country from many points of view, and its long military history has provided an unequaled opportunity for the development of weapons and fighting arts. With nearly two thousand years for the Japanese cultural penchant for organizing and refining to act upon these arts, the results today are a number of highly specialized disciplines, including jujutsu, judo, aikido, karatedo, kenpo, iaido, kendo, batto-jutsu and numerous others. All have long historical roots, systematized training methods, and a philosophical component, but none are older than jujutsu (considered the mother of all modern Japanese fighting arts) and iaido. Many historians argue that it is impossible to study the history of Japan without studying the history of its swords.

Indeed, swords have existed in Japan for its entire historical period, if we can believe the archeological evidence. Short, straight swords imported from China and Korea are among the earliest weapons found in historical sites around Japan. After 200 B.C., when these swords first appeared, the Japanese began making their own, and by around 700 A.D. they would be making the first of what are now considered the finest swords ever made anywhere in the world.

The person considered responsible for making the first vast improvements in Japanese sword design and manufacture was a smith named Amakuni. Like others in his profession, he was responding to the huge demand for weapons made by local, provincial and national leaders. There were almost constant regional conflicts over land rights and issues of power and, when not warring among themselves, it seems the early Japanese were invading the Korean peninsula, China, or defending against invaders from those places. Any leader with a supply of superior weapons would have been at a great advantage, so there was a constant, long-term effort to find sword makers who could improve the craft. The most devoted smiths made the quest for the perfect blade into a lifetime's pursuit, and there are men today who still devote their lives to this art.

The long sword in Japan has seen three major incarnations, and for each type of sword there has been a fighting style to match its shape. The early blades, called *chokuto* or "straight swords," tended to get longer as metallurgy techniques improved and, though not many specifics are known about the methods of wielding these weapons, the extra length without any significant increase in weight certainly provided a reach advantage for their owners. The handle size of these blades suggests that they were held in one hand, and the proliferation of two-edged blades suggests a thrusting and hacking fighting style common to two-edged blade fighting around the world.

The first major change in the shape of the sword came during Amakuni's time, perhaps made by Amakuni himself. It was found that a curved sword could be drawn from the scabbard more quickly and could provide a more effective cutting angle, so forging methods were developed to make a curved blade at least as strong as the earlier straight ones. These swords, called *tachi*, were extremely long, some nearing four feet, and were generally used by soldiers on horseback. The long, curved blade was ideal for a sweeping draw and slash against opponents on the ground or mounted upon other horses.

直
刀

太
刀

Later in Japan's history, most soldiers found themselves doing battle on foot, or engaging in individual combat against one another. For such men, the tachi were too long to be drawn or wielded comfortably, so a shorter sword was developed. This sword was the *katana*, and it is the sword that most modern iaido systems employ in practice. Katana are generally between two and four feet in length and, though curved, have a less pronounced arc than the tachi. They can be efficiently drawn from the scabbard into position for a horizontal, diagonal or vertical cut, and the curve of the blade lends itself well to the efficient slashing cut characteristic of iaido.

Evidence exists that swordsmen were engaging in single combat in Japan up until the Meiji Restoration in 1868. After the Restoration, swordsmanship went into a general decline, but there were a number of schools that perpetuated the art, usually called *iaijutsu*, *kenjutsu* or *batto-jutsu* at that time. The emphasis in these schools was preservation of the techniques that swordsmen had practiced before 1868.

As the society gradually adapted itself to the new, peaceful era, teachers of the martial arts began to reconsider the spiritual benefits of training in budo and to make these the primary focus of their teaching. Though it is true that Zen and other philosophical doctrines had always been a part of the education of the samurai, after all practical need for fighting skills had disappeared some teachers realized that, just as certain concepts from these doctrines could inspire in a warrior a better state of mind for doing battle, correct practice of the art in the absence of war naturally gives rise to the state of mind that is sought by practitioners of Zen. It had also been noted that long-time practitioners of the fighting arts often became the most insightful and gentle of human beings. So it was that many budo schools began to teach that martial arts training was not a means of learning how to fight, but a tool for perfecting the character of its students. The motto of the Eishin-Ryu Iaido system expresses this same thought:

> *Iai does not enable one to kill people,*
> *it is not meant for taking lives.*
> *It is expressly for the purpose of putting one's own life*
> *on a peaceful course.*

The most recent chapter in this conversion from fighting method to philosphical art form came after World War II, when the occupying forces of the United States forbade the Japanese from practicing their traditional fighting arts. In their efforts to get permission to practice again, various associations of teachers wrote new bylaws specifying that their arts were not meant for the taking of human life, but were means of preserving traditional culture and educating people. In concert with this effort, and with the overall change in emphasis in training, many schools changed the name of their arts. While they originally used the suffix *jutsu*, which means "art" or "technique," these schools began to employ the suffix *do*, which means "path" or "way." Thus jujutsu became judo, kenjutsu became kendo, and iaijutsu became iaido. The connotation of the "do" ending is that the art form is a way of life, a training method with philosophical benefits that extend to every aspect of an individual's makeup and have a profound effect for his or her entire lifespan.

Concepts which supplement the spiritual training of the martial artist have found their way into our modern budo vocabulary. *Kiai*, or the union of spiritual energies, is well known. *Zanshin*, the visible and invisible presence of spiritual energy, is another concept central to correct practice. *Reishiki*, etiquette, is vital to keep practice safe and efficient. Bushido, the code of the samurai, infuses all aspects of martial arts training. Without these and other concepts to guide training, Japanese martial arts become little more than physical fitness or fighting methods, and practice of the archaic arts such as iaido and kyudo, which offer no self-defense applications, would be difficult to justify. As historical art forms, however, with the cultural aspects intact, these arts are rewarding to practice for an entire lifetime.

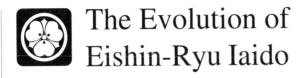

The Evolution of Eishin-Ryu Iaido

英信流歴史

The full name of the style of iaido that is the most widely practiced in central Japan today is Muso Jikiden Eishin-Ryu (moo-SEW GEE-KEY-den AY-shin re-ooh), meaning "Peerless, Direct Transmission, True-Faith Style." Eishin-Ryu claims a lineage about 450 years long, making it the second oldest extant martial art form in Japan. (The only budo form with a longer history is Tenshin Shoden Katori Shinto-Ryu, an eclectic system of fighting arts that includes some iaijutsu.) The founder of Eishin-Ryu was a man named Hayashizaki Jinsuke Minamoto Shigenobu, who lived between 1546 and 1621 in present-day Kanagawa Prefecture.

Many of the historical details of Hayashizaki's life are suspect since, like most famous martial artists in Japan, his story has been widely fictionalized, but it seems clear that he grew up during a time of constant warfare in Japan, and was exposed to various sword-fighting methods from an early age. It is said that he went to Yamagata Prefecture to pray for guidance and received divine inspiration for a new way of drawing the sword. Whatever the circumstances, at some point in middle age he established his own style of swordsmanship and called it Shimmei Muso-Ryu ("Divinely Inspired, Unparalleled Style").

Hayashizaki's iaido has had many names since then, as it has been passed down from teacher to student until the present day. It is considered the foundation for the two major styles of iaido that are practiced today: Eishin-Ryu and Muso Shinden-Ryu. In each generation a headmaster, or *soke* (SO-keh) has been appointed to guide the practice of the art, and each soke has had his own influence on its development. Eishin-Ryu claims an unbroken line of transmission from Hayashizaki Jinsuke through twenty-one generations to the present-day soke, Fukui Torao, who was appointed in 1992 by his predecessor, Kono Hyakuren. The names of all the headmasters from the founder's time are as follows:

Hayashizaki Jinsuke Minamoto Shigenobu, Founder
Tamiya Heibei Narimasa, 2nd generation
Nagano Muraku Nyudo, 3rd generation
Momo Gumbei Mitsushige, 4th generation
Arikawa Shozaemon Munetsugu, 5th generation
Banno Denemon no Jo Nobusada, 6th generation
Hasegawa Mondonosuke Eishin, 7th generation
Arai Seitetsu Seishin, 8th generation
Hayashi Rokudayu Morimasa, 9th generation
Hayashi Yasudayu Seisho, 10th generation
Oguro Motoemon Kiyokatsu, 11th generation
Hayashi Masu no Jo Masanari, 12th generation
Yoda Manzo Takakatsu, 13th generation
Hayashi Yadayu Masataka, 14th generation
Tanimura Kame no Jo Takakatsu, 15th generation
Goto Masasuke, 16th generation
Oe Masamichi, 17th generation
Hogiyama Namio, 18th generation
Fukui Harumasa, 19th generation
Kono Hyakuren, 20th generation
Fukui Torao, 21st generation

Most iaido historians agree that the inspiration for the name Eishin-Ryu came from the name of the seventh generation head-master, Hasegawa Chikaranosuke Eishin. Certainly the characters used in his name are the same as those used the name of the style. After the eleventh generation, the lineage split into two separate lines, one leading to Saito Isamu, the eighteenth generation head-master of the Muso Shinden-Ryu, and the other to Fukui Torao, as shown above. There also are a number of other, less-widely practiced, forms of iaido that grew out of Hayashizaki Jinsuke's art.

Today, Eishin-Ryu is practiced by two or three thousand people in Japan, and has exponents around the world. The administration of the system is primarily handled by the Eishin-Ryu Traditions Association, led by the soke, and by the All Japan Iaido Federation, which oversees competitions and promotions in many different iaido styles. An annual meeting of the All Japan Iaido Federation takes place in Kyoto, during which iaidoka from all over the country gather to demonstrate their skills. Some Eishin-Ryu has found its way overseas, as well, mostly through the efforts of the Kokusai Budoin, IMAF (International Martial Arts Federation), but the number of practitioners outside of Japan remains small.

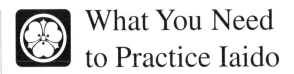

What You Need to Practice Iaido

居合刀

Iaido is a bit more expensive to begin practicing than many other martial arts because the student must have a practice sword. Otherwise, the requirements are simple: only a *hakama* and *gi* top are necessary to begin. Some schools start their students out with *bokuto* (wooden swords), making the initial investment lower, but eventually most students decide to obtain all the specialized equipment. Besides a large, open space in which to practice, the following items are included in the full complement of iaido gear:

> **Iaito.** The iaito is a full length sword, usually a little lighter than a real katana, but seldom sharp. It is crafted to simulate the balance and feel of the katana, and many have grooves cut into them which cause them to make a whistling sound when swung through the air. Some students use real swords in their practice, but this is not recommended for beginners since, in the first two or three years of practice, the risk of ruining an expensive blade is quite high.

Cleaning kit and oil. The iaito blade should be wiped off after every practice session and a light coat of oil applied. With real swords, the oil helps to prevent tarnishing. With iaito, it allows the blade to slide smoothly through the fingers during practice, and gradually builds up in the scabbard, facilitating smooth and silent drawing of the sword. The oil used in Japan is lightly scented with cloves.

Montsuki. This is the kimono-like top commonly worn during formal events by men and women in Japan. A *mon* is a Japanese crest, usually a family symbol. *Tsuki* means "attached." The color of the montsuki worn by an iaidoka is usually determined by the season—black in winter and white in summer—though black is always worn at formal events, such as tests or forms competitions.

Obi. The obi is a wide cloth belt wrapped around the outside of the montsuki at waist level. The katana is inserted between the layers of cloth, which help keep it from slipping away from the body.

Hakama. The hakama is the pleated skirt worn by martial artists in aikido, kendo, kyudo and other forms of budo. Black is the preferred color for a beginner in most arts.

Tabi. In most systems, these split-toed socks are reserved for for the most senior teachers. In the All Japan Iaido Federation, for example, only those of eighth dan ranking or above are allowed to wear tabi at formal events. Some students wear them during practice in winter to keep their feet warm.

There are other things that can be helpful in iaido, such as a knee pad for the left knee, since it is often in contact with the floor, and a cloth cover and leather carrying case for the sword. Some sort of undergarment is usually worn beneath the hakama, similar to long underwear used in North America, and under the mon-tsuki. There are actually specialized under garments for this purpose, though it is not required to have them.

About the Japanese Sword

日本刀

$\mathbf{T}$he Japanese sword is almost legendary among weapons collectors around the world, and with good reason. It is the strongest sword, for its weight, ever made, is capable of holding the sharpest edge, has the most elegant profile, and its fittings are exceptionally beautiful and carefully matched to the blade. Samurai warriors often imagined that their swords were possessed by some kind of spirit, and some enthusiastic modern storytellers have even described the visions of blood and heroism that leapt to mind when they held a famous blade.

For the iaido practitioner it is useful to note the unique curve of the blade and the matching profile of the scabbard. This curve is what allows the sword to be drawn quickly and directly into a position for offensive or defensive action. The wood of the scabbard, too, has its influence on the way the sword is drawn and replaced in the scabbard. Because of the softness of the wood, which cushions the blade and absorbs oil to protect it from rust, the sword must be wielded very lightly whenever it makes contact with the scabbard. The length of the typical katana handle is just long enough for a wide two-hand grip and, in a well-made weapon, balances the sword well enough to make one-handed swordplay possible. The weight and exact shape of the other fittings play a role in the balance of the sword as well. Everything about it must be functionally perfect and, at the same time, beautiful.

There are many books devoted to describing the making of Japanese sword, so a short description will be adequate here. Sword-making in Japan is a traditional art, and like other traditional arts requires long practice to learn and years to master. The most traditional of swordsmiths typically gathered iron-rich sand from certain areas in Japan and smelted the iron from it themselves. They then had various methods of adding carbon and refining the iron into steel. Few active swordsmiths follow all the traditional methods,

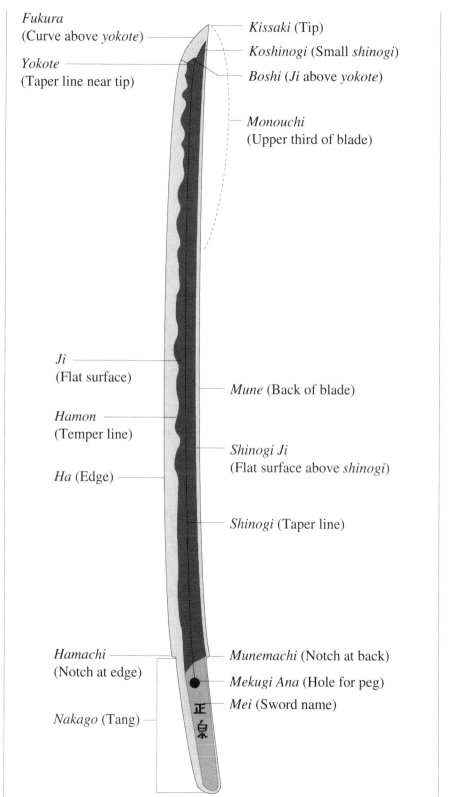

Fukura
(Curve above *yokote*)

Yokote
(Taper line near tip)

Kissaki (Tip)

Koshinogi (Small *shinogi*)

Boshi (*Ji* above *yokote*)

Monouchi
(Upper third of blade)

Ji
(Flat surface)

Mune (Back of blade)

Hamon
(Temper line)

Shinogi Ji
(Flat surface above *shinogi*)

Ha (Edge)

Shinogi (Taper line)

Hamachi
(Notch at edge)

Munemachi (Notch at back)

Mekugi Ana (Hole for peg)

Mei (Sword name)

Nakago (Tang)

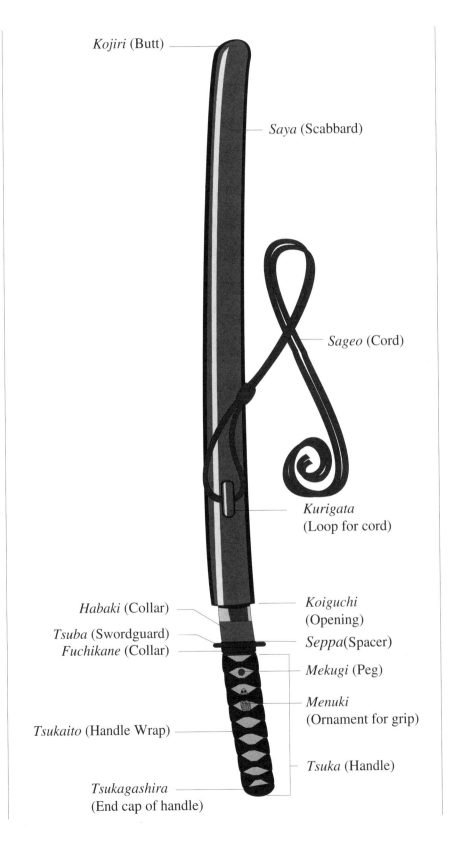

Kojiri (Butt)

Saya (Scabbard)

Sageo (Cord)

Kurigata
(Loop for cord)

Habaki (Collar)

Koiguchi
(Opening)

Tsuba (Swordguard)

Seppa(Spacer)

Fuchikane (Collar)

Mekugi (Peg)

Menuki
(Ornament for grip)

Tsukaito (Handle Wrap)

Tsuka (Handle)

Tsukagashira
(End cap of handle)

but all still fold their steel into hundreds or thousands of layers, which eventually lines up the molecules of the metal in such a way as to produce an extremely hard metal that holds a very sharp edge. There are a number of crucial aspects to making a good sword, and among these are obtaining exactly the right carbon content, enveloping a softer, more flexible core of metal in a harder jacket of metal that will constitute the sharp edge, hammering out the curve of the blade without bending it, and tempering the blade to make it a unified, beautiful work of art and an effective weapon.

Once the sword is finished, most smiths send it out to a sword-polisher, who specializes in shaping and sharpening the blade. Other men create the scabbard and fittings, and each step can take a month or more to complete. The Japanese government today carefully regulates the sword-making industry and, to protect against shabby workmanship, allows a swordsmith to produce no more than one blade a month. It is possible for smiths to make three or four times that number and still maintain quality standards, since they now use power hammers to shape the steel and have various other work-saving technologies, but the rules were set many years ago before these refinements. While it is not necessary for the iaido practitioner to understand how a sword is made, it can be a fascinating study. It is important, however, for a student of the art to have a general understanding of the parts of the sword and their functions.

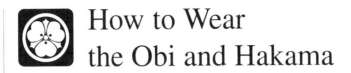

How to Wear the Obi and Hakama

The montsuki is worn with the left lapel over the right and the obi is worn over it, acting both as a means of securing it and as a means of support for the hakama. Place one end of the obi on the left side of the body, at about the height of the hipbone (1). Wrap the obi around the body from left to right (two or more times around), until there is just enough of the other end remaining to tie the knot (2). Some will find they must fold the end back over on itself to get it to just the right length. Bring the end around from the left side and tuck it under all the other layers of the obi, from bottom to top (3), then fold the tab that protrudes from below over toward the right. Fold the end down over it (4).

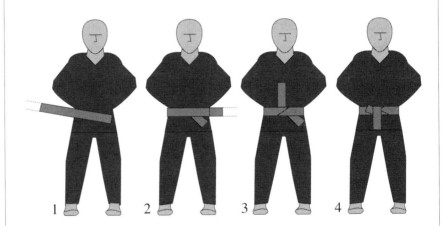

1   2   3   4

Pull the end back up through the loop formed with the tab, and pull both tight to form the knot (5). Slide the tied obi around on the body until the knot is in the center of the back (6). It is usually best to slide it from left to right, since that direction keeps the montsuki tight on the body.

The obi should be worn at the height of the hipbones. You will have to experiment with different degrees of tightness to strike a

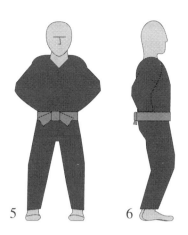

balance between comfort and control of the sword (since the sword is held in place mainly by the obi). It also takes some practice to keep the knot small and neat, but it is natural for the hakama to protrude from the back slightly due to the thickness of the knot. This is a good time to make sure that the undergarment is not bunched up under the obi.

Hold the hakama up by the front panel and step through the legs. Place the front band just below the top of the obi (7). Wrap the two bands around the body, just above the hip crest in back, so that the end that wraps around from the left goes over the other end (8). Fold the end that wraps from right to left up over the other end and tie them together at the back of the body (9). Lift the back panel up and place it against the back, just above the knot created by the bands from the front panel (10).

Wrap the ends around the front of the body, left over right as with the front (11). Tuck the end that wraps around from the left under all the other bands, including the bands from the front panel, from bottom to top (12). Tie the two bands from the front panel in the same manner as you tied the obi (13). Tuck the ends into the sides by winding them around the two bands from the front panel, but do not wind them around the band from the front panel (14). That band

21

must be left free for proper insertion of the sword. After the hakama is properly tied, reach inside it and adjust the montsuki by pulling down on the ends of the lapels. The montsuki should fit neatly inside the obi.

To insert the sheathed sword into the belt, begin from the top front and slide the butt of the scabbard underneath the layers of the obi. If the obi wraps three times or more around the body, the scabbard can be placed between the layers. In any case, the scabbard is slid through the obi, underneath the band of the back panel of the hakama and above the other bands (where the ends have been wrapped around them). Looking down at the sword at this point, the tsuba should be centered relative to the body. The sword should rest comfortably at a slight downward angle as in the illustration.

Etiquette and the Code of the Samurai

One of the first tasks facing any leader of fighting men is that of instilling discipline in his troops. This was especially important for the Japanese, since the samurai were part of an elite social group and were expected to deport themselves in accordance with their position. They were schooled in Confucian classics and taught how to behave within the rigid guidelines of Japan's ruling class. Any transgression of the rules was considered a serious problem, since every warrior in the retinue of a leader was considered a representative of his master. A breach of etiquette could easily lead to a duel, and hence death, or to war between two factions.

The close relationship between etiquette and the proper bearing of a martial artist is something that is not well understood today. Most people who practice martial arts assume that the concept of *reishiki* (etiquette) extends no further than the bow at the beginning of practice, or the use of the title *sensei* for their teacher. With this limited understanding of the concept, it is easy to see why such people don't realize how closely linked etiquette is to bushido, the code of the samurai. The word bushido calls to mind warriors making great efforts to serve their lords in times of trouble. During famine, a samurai might not have eaten for weeks because his master needed the food for some other purpose. He might have walked a hundred miles overnight to deliver an important message. One of the most common stories from feudal times is of some samurai fighting a gallant battle in his lord's name, only to be slain at the end.

Of course, it is not the aim of the warrior to die. His aim is to help his side win and, for that, his every action during combat must be correct. Any mistake means death. Constant vigilance is required; any expression of fear or self-interest leads to disaster. On the battlefield, bushido means doing what is correct at every moment, regardless of one's feelings. The most successful warriors are those who can focus their attention completely on the task at hand. This is the discipline of the battlefield.

Since battles seldom continue for more than a short time, however, the question then becomes: how does a leader instill this discipline in his men when there is no battle? There are mock battles, of course, and all sorts of military exercises that help to teach the principles of combat, but instilling the correct attitude is extremely difficult.

For the samurai, it turned out, a tool for teaching the correct attitude was already in place. Bushido was not confined to the battlefield, but actually governed their existence twenty-four hours a day. In times of peace, since every action was relevant to the status of their clan, it was required that they behave impeccably. In everyday society, this was nothing other than the application of reishiki, or correct etiquette. They had to do what was correct at all times, regardless of their feelings. Behaving this way day after day, with many social pressures reminding them of the importance of correct action, they eventually developed an ability to sense what was correct, and an aptitude for doing it. In fact, it is hard to imagine a better definition of character improvement—the commonly stated purpose of martial arts training—than this: *learning to sense what is correct, and developing an aptitude for doing it.* This is what budo is supposed to teach. The tools for teaching it have existed as long as have the samurai. Since, however, we live in a relatively peaceful society, the battlefield aspect is not available to us, so the peacetime aspect, reishiki, becomes all the more important.

The most obvious expression of etiquette in the dojo is the *rei*, or bow. There are many other facets as well, such as correct and safe handling of the sword, proper treatment of training partners, maintenance of equipment, and decorum. Each is one aspect of the larger general picture, which is harder to teach since it is more abstract. Actually understanding the principle is the goal, but not every student can make such progress. It is most important, for safety in practice and setting the correct example, however, that a student behave correctly. The basics, besides the rules of good manners that apply anywhere, are correct bowing and correct sword handling.

Basic Techniques

How to Bow

All traditional martial arts practice begins and ends with the bow. The bow (*rei*) is a symbol of respect for the traditions and humility in the face of the great teachers that necessarily precede one in the art. Bowing to another person does not indicate that one is worshipping that person, as some students of the martial arts have complained. Instead, the bow shows that both parties are willing to put aside any differences and cooperate in practice for a time. The rei also serves to denote the start and end of practice so that everyone involved is prepared to begin. It is easy to imagine the disastrous consequences if a student of iaido simply pulled out his sword and began practicing without giving any warning to the others in the group.

There are three major types of bow in the Eishin-Ryu Iaido system: the standing bow to the *shomen* (the front of the room, where some objects or pictures representing the traditions of the art are kept, called the *kamiza*, meaning "upper seat"), the seated bow to another person or to the teacher, and the seated bow to the sword. In all three, the sword is temporarily moved from a "live" position to a "safe" position to indicate the swordsman's lack of aggressive intent. As a part of understanding the overall use and strategy of the sword, it is important to understand when the sword is in a position to be used and when it is not. Whenever the scabbard is held in the left hand, making the handle of the sword available to the right hand, the sword can be drawn, so any such position is considered aggressive or, at the very least, alert (virtually all swordsman are right-handed). Whenever the sword is in a position that would make it difficult to draw (held by the scabbard in the right hand, for example), the swordsman is considered non-aggressive, and this position is used for most bows.

This is similar to the display position for swords on a rack: the handle points to the left. One way to decide whether or not a school is worth attending is by checking the position of any swords on display. If the handles point to the right, there's a good chance that the head of the school lacks knowledge of traditional swordsmanship.

In the standing bow, one holds the sword by the scabbard in the left hand. One then deliberately moves it out of this aggressive position by turning the handle toward the right, grasping the scabbard in the right hand, and finally holding the sword at the right side of the body with the right hand, handle pointing backwards, completely out of reach. The bow is performed with the sword remaining in this position and only after the bow is the weapon moved back into the left hand.

In the seated bow, performed in front of another person or a teacher, the sword is again moved from the left hand to the right hand, and this time set down at the right side of the body with the handle forward, directly in front of the right hand in a position from which it would be difficult to draw. When this bow is complete, the sword is usually moved directly into position for the *torei* (bowing to the sword), without being put in an aggressive position in between.

During the torei, the sword is placed directly in front of the student with the handle to the left, a non-aggressive position. It is also worth noting that the *omote*, or "face" of the sword, is down when it is set properly for the torei. Though the two sides of the blade may seem identical, the side which faces the left when the sword is held in two hands (or faces the kurigata when inserted in the scabbard), is considered the front, and that is the side shown when the blade is displayed on a rack. When the omote is down during the torei, the cutting edge faces the practitioner, so there is no danger of offending anyone facing him by pointing the edge in their direction. Paying close attention to all these details helps develop a keen awareness of the blade's position; a necessary skill for an iaidoka.

One can detect the influence that the sword arts have had on other martial arts by watching traditional practitioners of aikido and karate when they bow. Most aikido teachers, and many karate teachers, bow by moving their left hand down to the mat surface before the right hand. This is an emulation of the early swordsman, who wanted to keep the right hand ready in case some danger arose during the course of the bow. By retaining the older tradition, these teachers focus on the readiness aspect of the bow, cultivating alertness in their students.

The correct attitude to have during the bow is one of relaxed alertness, mixed with humility. Bowing is a time to focus concentration and to put aside thoughts of other matters, since wielding a sword is dangerous and requires one's full attention. When bowing to the kamiza or to the teacher, remember that no practice would be possible at all without the traditions and the teaching lineage that lead to you. Always rise from a bow a second later than the teacher and any senior students to show respect for their higher position. Try to maintain an awareness of your immediate environment on all sides. Awareness is one of the most important qualities of a swordsman!

Bowing Toward the Kamiza

Shinzen no Rei

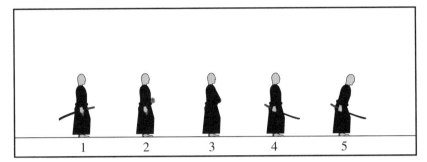

To begin practice, bow toward the kamiza, or *shomen*, to show respect for the traditions of the art.

1. Stand facing the kamiza, heels together with feet pointing 45° away from each other. The back should be straight and shoulders should be pulled back and down. Hold the sword in the left hand, near the top of the scabbard, with the edge upwards. Be sure to hold the tsuba with the thumb to keep the sword from slipping. The cord, or *sageo*, should be looped into thirds and held between the first and middle fingers of the left hand (with the middle, ring, and little fingers all inside the loop).

2. Move the sword to the front of the body. It should be held parallel to the ground with the edge still up.

3. Grasp the sword with the right hand, just past the left hand on the scabbard. Be sure to grasp the sageo as well.

4. Rotate the sword a half turn toward you, then move it to the right side of the body. The tip should end facing forward and down, and the edge should be downwards.

5. Bow by moving the body forward from the waist. Be sure not to move the sword during the bow. Always hold the bow slightly longer than any senior iaidoka.

6. Straighten the body.

7. Move the sword to the front of the body with the right hand. It should be held parallel to the ground with the edge still down.

8. Put the three smaller fingers of the left hand through the loop of the sageo (near the tsuba) and grasp the saya in the original position of the left hand. The thumb holds the tsuba.

9. Rotate the sword a half turn toward you. The sageo should drop into its original loop. Move the sword to the left side of the body, edge up. The standing bow is complete.

Seated Bows

Zarei

座
礼

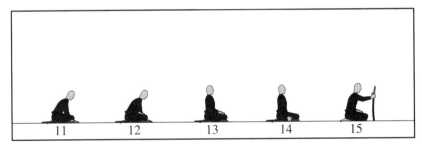

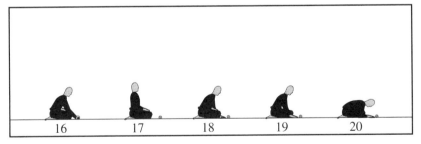

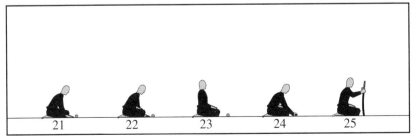

After bowing toward the kamiza, bow to show respect for the teacher and for the weapon. These bows are done from a seated position. All seated bows are called *zarei*.

1. Sit in seiza, with the knees two fist lengths apart (slightly closer for women). The left big toe should be on top of the right big toe. The katana is held in the left hand, the sageo looped in thirds between the first and middle fingers, with the thumb holding the tsuba. The sword should rest lightly on the left thigh, near the hip joint. The right hand rests, fingers together, just above midway up the right thigh, pointed slightly inwards. Shoulders should be pulled back and down, the back should be straight. The chin should be pulled in and the head should be held in a naturally erect position, as if suspended from the top by a string.

2. Move the butt of the sword forward, directly toward the centerline of the body.

3. Grasp the loop of the sageo with the middle, ring and little fingers of the right hand while taking the saya in the right hand. Replace the left thumb on the tsuba with the right.

4. Move the left hand back to press against the saya near the hip. Press with the hand held flat to control the movement of the saya.

5. Lift the sword with the right hand.

6. Place the sword on the floor near the right side of the body. The butt faces forward and the *omote*, or face of the sword, is down.

7. Move both hands onto the thighs, fingers together. The hands should be just above midway up the thighs and should point slightly inward. Wait for the teacher to initiate the bow before beginning.

8. Begin the bow by moving the body forward from the waist. The left hand moves first, to a position in front of the left knee, fingers pointing inward at a 45° angle.

9. Continue the bow by moving the right hand into a position in front of the right knee, fingers pointing inward at a 45° angle.

10. Lower the body until the chest comes into contact with the thighs. Elbows should move all the way down to touch the ground. Be sure to hold the bow longer than the teacher.

11. Begin to rise. Lift the right hand first.

12. Continue to rise while lifting the left hand.

13. End the first bow by sitting in seiza with both hands on the thigh.

14. To bow to show respect for the weapon (torei), take up the sword in the right hand, at a position near the top of the saya. Place the thumb on the tsuba and the middle, ring and little fingers through the loop of the sageo before grasping the saya.

15. Lift the sword and move the end out to a position in front and to the right of the right knee.

16. Set the butt of the sword down so that the sword lies in front of the knees. Omote is down. There should be sufficient room between the knees and the sword for the hands to be placed in their bowing position. The tsuba should be even with the middle of the left knee. Lay the sageo down along the far side of the sword and loop it around the end.

17–23. If a teacher is present, wait until the bow is initiated to begin. When practicing alone, bow when ready according to the instructions given for steps **7–13**, above.

24. Take up the sageo between the first and middle fingers of the right hand, two-thirds down its length, to create a loop in it. Grasp the sword near the top of the saya with the thumb on the tsuba.

25. Stand the sword up in front of the centerline of the body.

26. Move the left hand out to a position about a third of the way up the sword's length from the floor.

27. Slide the left hand down to the end of the sword and grasp the saya there.

28. Move the end with the left hand to a position just in front of the left hipbone to prepare for sliding it into the obi.

29. Insert the end of the sword into the obi and slide it back until the butt is even with the centerline of the body.

30. Use the left hand to move the sageo over the sword where it intersects the obi. Bring the sageo underneath the sword in front, then tuck the ends into the ties of the hakama at a point in front of the body just below the sword itself. The ends tuck in from the top down.

31. Sit and wait for instructions to rise. Grasp the sword in the left hand at the top of the saya, with the thumb on the tsuba, before standing.

Fundamentals of Practice

Standing. To stand correctly, before a technique begins or while waiting, place the heels together with the feet pointing outward at an angle of about 45°. The knees should be slightly bent and the hips tucked forward. The shoulders must be pulled back and down, the arms relaxed at the sides and the fingers curved slightly inward with the thumbs pressing lightly against the inside of the first joint of the first finger. The head is held erect, with the chin tucked. The balance of the entire body should always be minutely forward in Iaido practice, as if the practitioner were about to spring forward. Be careful not to exaggerate this inclination; it should be nearly undetectable to an observer.

Moving. Whenever moving during practice, be sure to grasp the scabbard with the left hand, and to use the thumb to hold the tsuba. This will keep the sword from sliding out of the scabbard unexpectedly.

Sitting. To sit in seiza, bend the knees, bend forward from the waist and reach down between the legs with the right hand. Use the hand to flip the hakama out toward the sides before sitting, left side first, then right. Both knees can be placed on the ground at the same time (though they must be placed there softly, without hitting), or the right knee can be set down first, followed by the left.

In seiza, the knees are about two fist widths apart (slightly closer together for women). The big toe of the left foot is placed above the big toe of the right foot. The back is held straight with the shoulders pulled back and down. The hands are placed lightly on the thighs, just above a point midway up from the knees, with the fingers turned inward. The head is held erect, with the chin tucked. The balance should be centered over the hips, although the advanced student will maintain a slightly forward inclination to facilitate rising.

Drawing (*nukitsuke*).   The standard draw begins with the sword in the scabbard, left hand holding the scabbard near its top and the right hand grasping the handle of the sword close to the tsuba.

1. Rotate the sword and scabbard outward about 45°.

2. Begin drawing the butt slowly down center toward the level of the throat while continuing to rotate the sword and scabbard outward. Pull the scabbard back while drawing the sword. The angle of the blade should reach 90° just as the tip is about to clear the scabbard.

3. When the blade clears the scabbard, tighten the grip of the right hand to bring the sword parallel to the ground. Extend the right arm in a horizontal arc across the front of the body at shoulder level. Stop when the sword is pointing straight ahead. Shoulders must be squared, arm extended 45° to the right. Pull the scabbard back until it is stopped by the obi. The speed of this draw should gradually increase. Start out slowly, speeding up as the sword clears the scabbard until the cut moves very fast across the front of the body. Stop cleanly at the finished position without bouncing.

Blade   **Angle**

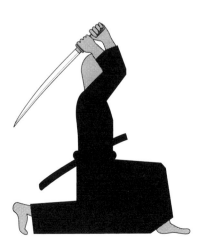

Raising the sword overhead (*furikaburi*). After many drawing or parrying motions, the sword must be raised over the head into a position for a downward cut. It is important to execute this motion properly to take advantage of its defensive possibilities. The motion begins in the wrist, which allows the sword to be put into a position to protect the head without bending the arm too much. The arm should stay in the "unbendable" position until the sword is fully overhead. Throughout this motion, the tip of the sword must be kept lower than the handle, to allow an opponent's sword to slide off without contacting one's own head or shoulder.

Another important checkpoint is that the *koshi* (the thickest third near the handle) of the sword, should not pass across the centerline of the body and head until the last moment. The koshi is the part of the sword which is always used to absorb or parry a downward strike from an opponent. The left hand should move smoothly up to grasp the end of the handle just as the sword moves into position over the head. The correct finishing position for this movement puts the tsuba even with the back of the head.

Holding the sword for cutting. Grasp the handle with both hands, right hand near the tsuba, left hand near the butt of the handle. For flexibility, apply more strength in the first and ring fingers and less

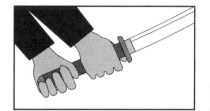

in the others. Both hands should rotate inward to place the palms nearly on top of the handle.

Cutting (*kirioroshi*). There are four major points that should be noted in a proper downward cut. Force must be applied along the entire edge of the blade, and the sword must be used to slice rather than hack at an object, as follows:

1. At the top of the cut, the elbows should be held wide apart. The tsuba should be even with the back of the head.

2. The elbows should be brought together during the cut, so the arms end in the "unbendable" position. The combination of the two elbow positions will force the sword to move in a slightly elliptical path, further away from the body at first, then closer near the end. The last third is where the slicing aspect is most pronounced.

3. Palms rotate inward on the handle. This can be awkward at first, but can be made easier by thinking of twisting the wrists toward each other. This forces the palms on top of the hilt and facilitates pressing down with both hands throughout the cut.

4. The left hand provides the power for the cut. The function of the right hand is mainly to steer the sword through a clean cutting line.

Flipping off the blood (*chiburi*). Since all the sword motions in iaido are based on real fighting methods, some account has to be taken of the real result of cutting a person: blood on the blade. The blood has to be cast off before the sword can be returned to the scabbard. After the cut, the sword is moved into a position near the temple, shown below. The hand is open at this point, so that the sword is held against the palm by the thumb of the right hand. The fingertips should touch the temple. The left hand, during this time, presses flat against the scabbard at the point where it passes through the obi, helping to stabilize it.

The chiburi motion is begun by moving the sword across the front of the face. The motion is propelled by closing the right hand and squeezing with the little, ring, and middle fingers. The blade should travel on a nearly vertical plane in front of the body, stopping with the tip slightly forward and near the floor, as shown. To be considered correct (and to have the most actual effect) the blade of the sword should be flat throughout this motion, edge always leading. A well-made sword or iaito will make a soft whistling sound during this motion if the angle of the blade is correct.

In this illustration, the chiburi is being started in a kneeling position. In order for there to be enough room to complete the motion, the practitioner stands up. Sometimes the same type of chiburi begins and ends in a standing position. There is another main type of chiburi, a side chiburi, which will be explained in detail later.

Returning the sword to the scabbard (*noto*).   It is important to practice the noto slowly and precisely at first to minimize wear on the scabbard. Try to slide the back of the sword along its mating surface with the scabbard, rather than the cutting edge.

1. Grasp the scabbard with the first finger and the thumb of the left hand extending past the opening of the scabbard. Place the sword on the opening between the two fingers fifteen centimeters (six inches) down the blade from the tsuba. The angle of the blade should be about 60° from straight up and down.

2. Draw the sword away from the body at an angle of 45° until the tip just clears the opening between the fingers.

3. Insert the tip in the scabbard and begin moving the sword back into it. Keep the sword about level with the floor and on the 45° line. Let the left hand slide back after it is contacted by the tsuba, then place the thumb on the tsuba after the sword is fully seated in the scabbard. The angle of the blade gradually moves toward straight up and down until it reaches 30°.

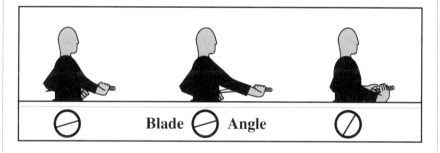

Blade **Angle**

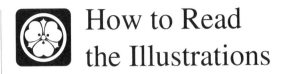

How to Read the Illustrations

For clarity, all illustrations of forms in this book are drawn so that important positions are shown from the side. The direction in which the swordsman should face is shown by the arrow which appears above the drawing. In the example below, the swordsman in position 1 is facing straight ahead (toward the *shomen* in ordinary practice), while the swordsman in positions 2 and 3 is facing right, relative to the shomen. If there were a front view drawing of those positions, the swordsman would be facing the reader. Though the turn itself cannot be shown in a two-dimensional drawing, it will be described in the explanation which accompanies the drawing. In position 4, the swordsman is facing left, or away from the reader, in 5 and 6, the rear, just as shown, and in 7, the front again.

The arrows showing direction appear above only the first position for a new direction. All subsequent positions take place facing the same direction, until a new arrow appears. The arc shows the direction in which the swordsman has turned to reach the new position.

⬢ Seated Set

The techniques of the Seated Set *(Seiza no Bu)* not surprisingly, are mainly those of moving out of the seiza position and into an offensive or defensive position. At the same time, all the major sword motions encountered in more advanced sets are found in this basic set, which explains why most teachers of iaido consider this the most important set of all. Many students are required to spend two or three years practicing the drawing and cutting motions of the seiza forms before being introduced to other material, and serious practice of these techniques pays great dividends in terms of the students' progress.

In the seiza position, and in the kneeling positions that follow it, the back must be kept very straight, the shoulders must be squared and pulled down at all times, the chin must be pulled in, and the upper body must ride smoothly atop the hips and legs to maintain optimum balance. These techniques are an excellent tool for developing leg strength, a healthy lower back, and good balance. It is far more important to practice them slowly, with concentration and attention to detail, than it is to try to demonstrate a lot of speed or power in practice. The names of the seiza forms are as follows:

1.	Forward	*Mae*	44
2.	Right	*Migi*	47
3.	Left	*Hidari*	50
4.	Rear	*Ushiro*	53
5.	Eightfold Fences	*Yaegaki*	57
6.	Parrying	*Ukenagashi*	62
7.	Assisting at Seppuku	*Kaishaku*	65
8.	Pursuit	*Tsukekomi*	68
9.	Moonbeams	*Tsukikage*	72
10.	Tailwind	*Oikaze*	76
11.	Sudden Draw	*Nukiuchi*	80

正座の部

One • Forward

Ippon Me • Mae

前

Scenario. A swordsman faces an opponent. Both are seated. As the opponent prepares to attack, the swordsman quickly draws and cuts him across the throat, then finishes him with a downward cut. Flipping the blade to remove any blood, the swordsman resheathes his sword and stands up in a dignified manner.

1. Sit in seiza, facing forward, with the back straight, chin tucked, hands flat on thighs and fingers together.

2. Grasp the scabbard with the left hand. Place the thumb on the tsuba to prevent the sword from slipping.

3. Grasp the handle of the sword, near the tsuba, with the right hand. Rotate the edge of the sword outward about 30° while moving the knees together.

4. Begin to draw the sword directly ahead and toward throat level while rising onto the knees. Move onto the balls of the feet. Use the left hand to pull the scabbard back toward the obi. Rotate the edge of the sword to 90° (flat) just before position 5.

5. Draw the sword on a horizontal line in front of the body. Simultaneously step out with the right leg. The finished position should be as follows: shoulders square; right arm extended toward the right front corner, level with the floor. The blade should be level, pointing straight ahead.

6. Bring the sword overhead, keeping the tip lower than the handle throughout the motion. Move the left hand up to grasp the handle.

7. Slide the right foot slightly forward.

8. Cut down center. Stop the sword in a position such that the butt of the handle is one fist length from the abdomen. Pull in with the right foot while cutting, driving the hips forward to add power to the cut.

9. Extend the sword slightly forward without raising or lowering the tip. Rotate the blade 45° to the right. Open the right hand so that the sword is held between the thumb and the palm of the hand. Move the left hand to press against the scabbard where it intersects the obi.

10. Extend the sword in a horizontal circle, moving toward the right. When the arm and sword point toward the right front corner, let the sword swing around toward the rear and bend the right arm at the elbow, bringing the hand straight toward the temple. Stop when the fingers touch the temple.

11. Perform chiburi by whipping the sword in a circle across the front of the body. At the same time, stand up by stepping forward with the left foot. The left foot should stop about half a foot's length further back than the right, with the heel slightly raised. In the standing position, keep the knees bent, the hips low, and the feet pointing out 45°. The right arm should be slightly in front of the body, with the sword tip extended forward, toward the ground.

12. Slide the right foot back until it is about two full foot lengths behind the right. The right heel should be pressed downward, but should not touch the floor. Move the whole sword backward about one inch while stepping back, to complement the leg motion.

13. Grasp the scabbard in the left hand, making a cradle with the thumb and forefinger which extends past the opening of the scabbard.

14. Move the sword across the front of the body until it rests on the finger cradle about six inches from the tsuba. The sword should be level, its edge at an angle of 60°.

15. Slide the sword away from the body at a 45° angle until the tip reaches the opening of the scabbard. Keep it level.

16. Begin to slide the sword into the scabbard while slowly lowering the body onto the right knee. Both the sliding sword and the dropping motion should begin slowly and gradually decrease in speed. There should be no bump when the knee contacts the ground. Gradually rotate the edge of the blade toward straight up and down while sliding the sword into the scabbard. It should be at an angle of about 10° when the sword is fully seated in the scabbard. Let the left hand slide back when it is contacted by the scabbard. As soon as the sword is fully seated, place the thumb of the left hand on the tsuba.

17. Move the right hand to the butt of the handle and grasp it there.

18. Stand up by stepping forward with the right leg. The heels should be together, feet pointing outward 45°. Adjust the sword so that the handle meets the centerline of the body.

19. Move the right hand down to a relaxed position at the side of the body. Step back to the starting point, moving the left foot first.

Two · Right

Nihon Me · Migi

右

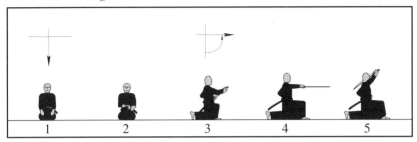

Scenario. The opponent sits facing the swordsman's left side. As the opponent prepares to attack, the swordsman quickly turns, draws and cuts him across the throat, then finishes him with a downward cut. Flipping the blade to remove any blood, the swordsman resheathes his sword and stands up in a dignified manner.

1. Sit in seiza, facing to the right.

47

2. Grasp the scabbard with the left hand. Place the thumb on the tsuba to prevent the sword from slipping.

3. Grasp the handle of the sword, near the tsuba, with the right hand. Rotate the edge of the sword outward about 30° while moving the knees together.

4. Rise onto the knees and onto the balls of the feet. Raise the handle of the sword slightly at the same time, to prepare for the draw.

5. Pivot 90° to face the shomen while drawing the sword toward throat level. The butt of the sword should point about 30° to the right. Use the left hand to pull the scabbard back toward the obi. Rotate the edge of the sword to 90° just before position 6.

6. Step out with the left leg while drawing the sword into a horizontal line across the front of the body. The finished position should be as follows: shoulders square; right arm extending forward and to the right front corner, level with the floor. The sword blade should be level, pointing straight ahead.

7. Bring the sword overhead, keeping the tip lower than the handle throughout the motion. Bring the left hand up to grip the handle at the same time.

8. Slide the left foot slightly forward.

9. Cut down center. Stop the sword in a position such that the butt of the handle is one fist length from the abdomen. Pull in with the left foot while making the cut in order to drive the hips forward, adding power to the cut.

10. Extend the sword forward without raising or lowering it. Rotate the edge about 45° to the right. Open the right hand so the sword is held between the thumb and the palm of the hand. Move the left hand to press against the scabbard where it intersects the obi.

11. Extend the sword in a circle moving toward the right. When the arm reaches a 45° angle from the body, let the sword swing around toward the rear and bend the right arm. Bring the hand straight toward the temple. Stop with the fingers touching the temple.

12. Perform chiburi by whipping the sword in a circle across the front of the body. Stand up during this motion by stepping forward with the right foot. The right foot should stop about half a foot's length back from the left. The right heel should be slightly raised. In the standing position, keep the knees bent, the hips low, and point the feet out 45°. The right arm should stop slightly in front of the body, with the tip of the sword extended forward and toward the ground.

13. Slide the left foot back until it is about two foot lengths behind the right. The left heel should be pressed downward but not touching the floor. Move the whole sword backwards about one inch while stepping back, to complement the leg motion.

14. Grasp the scabbard in the left hand, making a cradle with the thumb and forefinger, which extends past the opening of the scabbard.

15. Move the sword across the front of the body until it rests on the finger cradle at a point on the blade about six inches from the tsuba. The sword should be level, its edge at about a 60° angle.

16. Slide the sword away from the body at a 45° angle until the tip reaches the opening of the scabbard. Keep it level.

17. Begin to slide the sword into the scabbard while slowly lowering the body onto the left knee. Both motions should begin slowly and gradually decrease in speed. There should be no bump when the knee contacts the ground. Gradually rotate the edge of the blade toward straight up and down while sliding the sword into the scabbard. It should be at an angle of about 10° when the sword is fully seated in the scabbard. Let the left hand slide back when it is contacted by the tsuba. As soon as the sword is fully seated, place the thumb of the left hand on the tsuba.

18. Move the right hand to the butt of the handle and grasp it there.

19. Stand up by stepping forward with the left leg. The heels should be together, feet pointing outward 45°. Adjust the sword so that the handle meets the centerline of the body.

20. Move the right hand down to a relaxed position at the side of the body. Step back to the starting point (about three steps), moving the left foot first.

49

Three • Left

Sanbon Me • Hidari

Scenario. The opponent sits facing the swordsman's right side. As the opponent prepares to attack, the swordsman quickly turns, draws and cuts the opponent across the throat, then finishes him with a downward cut. Flipping the blade to remove any blood, the swordsman resheathes his sword and stands up in a dignified manner.

1. Sit in seiza, facing to the left.

2. Grasp the scabbard with the left hand. Place the thumb on the tsuba to prevent the sword from slipping.

3. Grasp the handle of the sword near the tsuba with the right hand. Rotate the edge of the sword outward about 30° while moving the knees together.

4. Rise onto the knees and the balls of the feet. Raise the handle of the sword slightly at the same time, to prepare for the draw.

5. Pivot 90° to face the shomen while drawing the sword toward throat level. The butt of the sword should point straight ahead. Use the left hand to pull the scabbard back toward the obi. Rotate the edge of the sword to 90° just before movement 6.

6. Step out with the right leg while drawing the sword into a horizontal line across the front of the body. The finished position should be as follows: shoulders square; right arm extended to the right front corner, level with the floor. The sword blade should be level, pointing straight ahead.

7. Bring the sword overhead, keeping the tip lower than the handle throughout the motion. Bring the left hand up to grip the handle at the same time.

8. Slide the right foot slightly forward.

9. Cut down center. Stop the sword in a position such that the butt of the handle is one fist length from the abdomen. Pull in with the right foot while making the cut, in order to drive the hips forward, adding power to the cut.

10. Extend the sword slightly forward without raising or lowering it. Rotate the edge about 45° to the right. Open the right hand so the sword is held between the thumb and the palm. Move the left hand to press against the scabbard where it intersects the obi.

11. Extend the sword in a circle moving toward the right. When the arm reaches a 45° angle from the body, let the sword swing around toward the rear and bend the right arm, bringing the hand straight toward the temple. Stop with the fingers touching the temple.

12. Perform chiburi by whipping the sword in a circle across the front of the body. Stand up during this motion by stepping forward with the left foot. The left foot should stop about half a foot's length back from the right. The left heel should be slightly raised. In the standing position, keep the knees bent, the hips low, and the feet pointing out 45°. The right arm should stop slightly in front of the body, with the tip of the sword extended toward the ground.

13. Slide the right foot back until it is about two foot lengths behind the left. The right heel should be pressed downward but not touching the floor. Move the whole sword backwards about one inch while stepping back to complement the leg motion.

14. Grasp the scabbard in the left hand, making a cradle with the thumb and forefinger which extends past the opening of the scabbard.

15. Move the sword across the front of the body until it rests on the finger cradle at a point on the blade about six inches from the tsuba. The sword should be level, its edge at about a 60° angle.

16. Slide the sword away from the body at a 45° angle until the tip reaches the opening of the scabbard. Keep it level.

17. Begin to slide the sword into the scabbard while slowly lowering the body onto the right knee. Both motions should begin slowly and gradually decrease in speed. There should be no bump when the knee contacts the ground. Gradually rotate the edge of the blade toward straight up and down while sliding the sword into the scabbard. It should be at an angle of about 10° when the sword is fully seated in the scabbard. Let the left hand slide back when it is contacted by the scabbard. As soon as the sword is fully seated, place the thumb of the left hand on the tsuba.

18. Move the right hand to the butt of the handle. Grasp the handle.

19. Stand up by stepping forward with the right leg. The heels should be together, feet pointing outward 45°. Adjust the sword so that the handle meets the centerline of the body.

20. Move the right hand down to a relaxed position at the side of the body. Step back to the starting point (about three steps), moving the left foot first.

Four • Rear

Yonhon Me • Ushiro

後

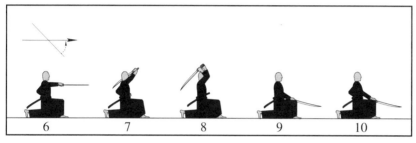

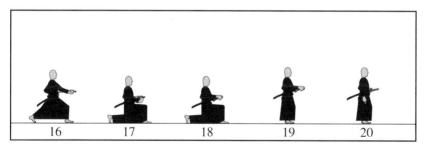

Scenario. An opponent sits facing the swordsman's back. As the opponent prepares to attack, the swordsman quickly turns, draws and cuts the opponent across the throat, then finishes him with a downward cut. Flipping the blade to remove any blood, the swordsman resheathes his sword and stands up in a dignified manner.

1. Sit in seiza, facing to the rear.

2. Grasp the scabbard with the left hand. Place the thumb on the tsuba to prevent the sword from slipping.

3. Grasp the handle of the sword, near the tsuba, with the right hand. Rotate the edge of the sword outward about 30° while moving the knees together.

4. Rise onto the knees and the balls of the feet. Raise the handle of the sword slightly at the same time, to prepare for the draw.

5. Pivot 135° on the right knee. The left knee should end up pointing 45° to the right, at the same angle as the body.

6. Draw toward throat level, 45° to the right of straight ahead. Slide the left foot back toward the right slowly while drawing. Use the left hand to pull the scabbard back toward the obi. Rotate the edge of the sword to 90° just before movement 6.

7. Step out with the left leg while cutting with the sword in a horizontal line across the front of the body. The finished position should be as follows: shoulders square; right arm extended to the right front corner, level with the floor. The sword blade should be level, pointing straight ahead.

8. Bring the sword overhead, keeping the tip lower than the handle, while bringing the left hand up to grip the handle.

9. Slide the left foot slightly forward.

10. Cut down center. Stop the sword in a position such that the butt of the handle is one fist's length from the abdomen. Pull in with the left foot while making the cut, in order to drive the hips forward, adding power to the cut.

11. Extend the sword slightly forward without raising or lowering it. Rotate the edge about 45° to the right. Open the right hand so that the sword is held between the thumb and the palm. Move the left hand to press against the scabbard where it intersects the obi.

12. Extend the sword in a circle moving toward the right. When the arm reaches a 45° angle from the body, let the sword swing around

toward the rear and bend the right arm, bringing the hand toward the temple. Stop with the fingers touching the temple.

13. Perform chiburi by whipping the sword in a circle across the front of the body. Stand up during this motion by stepping forward with the right foot. The right foot should stop about half a foot's length back from the left. The right heel should be slightly raised. In the standing position, keep the knees bent, the hips low, and the feet point out 45°. The right arm should stop slightly in front of the body, with the tip of the sword extended forward and toward the ground.

14. Slide the left foot back until it is about two foot lengths behind the right. The left heel should be pressed downward but not touching the floor. Move the whole sword backwards about one inch while stepping back to complement the leg motion.

15. Grasp the scabbard in the left hand, making a cradle with the thumb and forefinger which extends past the opening of the scabbard.

16. Move the sword across the front of the body until it rests on the finger cradle at a point on the blade about six inches from the tsuba. The sword should be level, its edge at about a 60° angle below straight up and down.

17. Slide the sword away from the body at a 45° angle until the tip reaches the opening of the scabbard. Keep it level.

18. Begin to slide the sword into the scabbard while slowly lowering the body onto the left knee. Both motions should begin slowly and gradually decrease in speed. There should be no bump when the knee contacts the ground. Gradually rotate the edge of the blade toward straight up and down while sliding the sword into the scabbard. It should be at an angle of about 10° when the sword is fully seated in the scabbard. Let the left hand slide back when it is contacted by the scabbard. As soon as the sword is fully seated, place the thumb of the left hand on the tsuba.

19. Move the right hand to the butt of the handle and grasp it there.

20. Stand up by stepping forward with the left leg. The heels should be together, feet pointing outward 45°. Adjust the sword so that the handle meets the centerline of the body.

21. Move the right hand down to a relaxed position at the side of the body. Step back to the starting point (about three steps), moving the left foot first.

Five • Eightfold Fences

Gohon Me • Yaegaki

八重垣

1   2   3   4   5

6   7   8   9   10

11   12   13   14   15

16   17   18   19   20

21   22   23   24   25

| 26 | 27 | 28 |

Scenario. The swordsman faces his opponent. Both are seated. As the opponent prepares to attack, the swordsman quickly draws and cuts him across the throat, then attempts to finish him. The opponent fades back to avoid the oncoming cut, so the swordsman moves foward while cutting. Flipping the blade to remove any blood from it, the swordsman begins to resheath his sword, but the opponent strikes at his leg. The swordsman blocks the cut and, this time, finishes his opponent. He then flips the blood off his sword, resheathes it, and stands up with dignity.

1. Sit in seiza, facing forward.

2. Grasp the scabbard with the left hand. Place the thumb on the tsuba to prevent the sword from slipping.

3. Grasp the handle of the sword, near the tsuba, with the right hand. Rotate the edge of the sword outward about 30° while moving the knees together.

4. Begin to draw the sword directly down center and toward throat level while rising onto the knees. Move onto the balls of the feet. Use the left hand to pull the scabbard back toward the obi. Rotate the edge of the sword to 90° just before movement 5.

5. Step out with the right leg while cutting with the sword in a horizontal line across the front of the body. The finished position should be as follows: shoulders squared, right arm extended forward and to the right at a 45° angle, level with the floor. The sword blade should be level, pointing straight ahead.

6, 7. Bring the sword overhead, keeping the tip lower than the handle throughout the motion, while standing up and stepping forward with the left leg. Bring the left hand up to the handle.

8. Step out with the left foot.

9. Cut straight down while dropping onto the right knee. Control the weight during the cut so that the knee touches the ground lightly.

10. Perform chiburi by flipping the blade out to the side with the right hand. Try to move the whole blade as one unit rather than moving the tip or handle first. In the finished position, the sword should be at hip level, about six inches away from the right leg. The tsuba should be just forward of the knee, blade level and pointing straight ahead. Move the left hand to press against the scabbard at the point where it intersects the obi.

11. Grasp the scabbard in the left hand, making a cradle with the thumb and forefinger which extends past the opening of the scabbard. Move the sword across the front of the body until it rests on the finger cradle at a point on the blade about six inches from the tsuba. The sword should be level, its edge at about a 60° angle below straight up and down.

12. Slide the sword away from the body at a 45° angle until the tip reaches the opening of the scabbard. Keep it level.

13. Begin to slide the sword into the scabbard while slowly moving the left foot back toward the right knee. Stop when the left foot is just behind the right knee and the tsuba contacts the left hand.

14. Begin standing up while drawing the sword straight ahead and level with the ground. Use the left hand to pull the scabbard back toward the obi.

15. As soon as the tip of the sword clears the scabbard, step back with the left foot while pressing down and to the right side quickly with the flat of the blade. The left foot should end directly behind the right foot, on a 45° angle with the heel on the floor. The tip of the sword should be close to the ground, about twelve inches from the toes of the right foot.

16. Bring the sword overhead while moving the left knee and shoulder forward. Set the left knee down next to the right foot. Move the left hand up to grasp the handle of the sword at the same time.

17. Slide the right foot slightly forward.

18. Cut down forward and center. Stop the sword in a position such that the butt of the handle is one fist length from the abdomen. Pull in with the right foot while making the cut, in order to drive the hips forward, adding power to the cut.

19. Extend the sword slightly forward without raising or lowering it. Rotate the edge about 45° to the right. Open the right hand so that the sword is held between the thumb and the palm. Move the left hand to press against the scabbard where it intersects the obi.

20. Extend the sword in a circle moving toward the right. When the arm and sword reach a 45° angle from the body, let the sword swing around toward the rear and bend the right arm at the elbow, bringing the hand straight toward the temple. Stop with the fingers touching the temple.

21. Perform chiburi by whipping the sword in a circle across the front of the body. Stand up during this motion by stepping forward with the left foot. The left foot should stop about half a foot's length further back than the right. The left heel should be slightly raised. In the standing position, keep the knees bent, the hips low, and the feet point out 45°. The right arm should stop slightly in front of the body, with the tip of the sword extended forward and toward the ground.

22. Slide the right foot back until it is about two foot lengths behind the left. The right heel should be pressed downward but not touching the floor. Move the whole sword backwards about one inch while stepping back to complement the leg motion.

23. Grasp the scabbard in the left hand, making a cradle with the thumb and forefinger which extends past the opening of the scabbard.

24. Move the sword across the front of the body until it rests on the finger cradle at a point on the blade about six inches from the tsuba. The sword should be level, its edge at about a 60° angle.

25. Slide the sword away from the body at a 45° angle until the tip reaches the opening of the scabbard. Keep it level.

26. Begin to slide the sword into the scabbard while slowly lowering the body onto the right knee. Both the sliding sword and the dropping motion should begin slowly and gradually decrease in speed. There should be no bump when the knee contacts the ground. Gradually rotate the edge of the blade toward straight up and down while sliding the sword into the scabbard. It should be at an angle of about $10°$ when the sword is fully seated in the scabbard. Let the left hand slide back when it is contacted by the scabbard. As soon as the sword is fully seated, place the thumb of the left hand on the tsuba.

27. Move the right hand to the butt of the handle. Grasp the handle at that point.

28. Stand up by stepping forward with the right leg. The heels should be together, feet pointing outward $45°$. Adjust the sword so that the handle meets the centerline of the body.

29. Move the right hand down to a relaxed position at the side of the body. Step back to the starting point (about three steps), moving the left foot first.

Six • Parrying
Roppon Me • Ukenagashi

受流

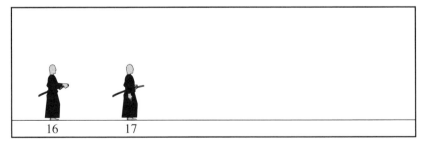

Scenario. The swordsman is seated. An opponent begins to approach from the left front. The swordsman stands and draws, parrying a cut by the opponent, and turns to finish him. He then spins the sword to flip the blood off, resheathes it, and stands up with dignity.

1. Sit in seiza, facing the right front corner (illustration shows direct side view for clarity).

2. Grasp the scabbard with the left hand. Place the thumb on the tsuba to prevent the sword from slipping.

3. Grasp the handle of the sword, near the tsuba, with the right hand. Move the knees together.

4. Rise onto the knees and move onto the balls of the feet.

5. Step out on the 45° line with the left leg. Draw the sword on the same line, level with the floor. Look straight toward the shomen.

6. Stand up and step out 45° to the right rear with the right foot. Draw the sword and lift it, keeping it level, to a defensive position overhead. The tip should be slightly lower than the handle, the widest third of the blade in front of the head, and the edge of the blade rotated 45° back.

7. Pull the left hip and shoulder sharply back and pivot on the right foot to face 45° left. Use the body motion to bring the sword into a position overhead. Move the left hand up to grasp the handle.

8. Step forward with the right leg while cutting straight down the 45° left direction. The right foot should end about a half foot's length behind the left, with the heel just off the ground.

9. Step back 45° toward the right rear with the left foot, bringing the left shoulder and hip into a position behind the right shoulder. Move the tip of the sword back until the monouchi rests on the right leg just above the knee. The edge should be perpendicular to the angle of the leg.

10. Switch the grip of the right hand so that the palm faces down.

11. Grasp the scabbard with the left hand, forming a cradle at the opening with the thumb and forefinger.

12. Swing the sword tip around in front of the body and rest the blade on the cradle created by the left hand. The point where the blade contacts the left hand should be about six inches from the tsuba.

13. Slide the sword away from the body at a 45° angle until the tip reaches the opening of the scabbard. Keep it level.

14. Begin to slide the sword into the scabbard while turning the body to bring the shoulders and hip back to square. Begin slowly lowering the body onto the left knee. Both the sliding sword and the dropping motion should begin slowly and gradually decrease in speed. There should be no bump when the knee contacts the ground. Gradually rotate the edge of the blade toward straight up and down while sliding the sword into the scabbard. It should be at an angle of about 10° when the sword is fully seated in the scabbard. Let the left hand slide back when it is contacted by the scabbard. As soon as the sword is fully seated, place the thumb of the left hand on the tsuba.

15. Move the right hand to the butt of the handle. Grasp the handle at that point.

16. Stand up by stepping forward with the right leg. The heels should be together, feet pointing outward 45°. Adjust the sword so that the handle meets the centerline of the body.

17. Move the right hand down to a relaxed position at the side of the body. Step back to the starting point (about three steps), moving the left foot first to adjust the body to face toward the shomen.

Seven • Assisting at Seppuku

Nanahon Me • Kaishaku

Scenario. A samurai prepares to commit seppuku (ritual suicide). His second sits behind him. The second stands and draws his sword to an overhead position. Once the samurai has cut his own belly, the second steps forward and beheads him, then spins the sword to flip the blood off, resheathes it, and stands up with dignity.

1. Sit in seiza, facing straight ahead.

2. Grasp the scabbard with the left hand. Place the thumb on the tsuba to prevent the sword from slipping.

3. Grasp the handle of the sword, near the tsuba, with the right hand. Do not close the knees completely in this form; rather, close the distance between them by about half.

4. Rise onto the knees and move onto the balls of the feet.

5. Step out with the right leg. Draw the sword across the front of the body, level with the floor. Stop when two thirds of the sword is out of the scabbard.

6. Stand up by stepping to the rear with the right foot. Draw the sword and lift it, keeping it level and parallel to the shoulders, to a position behind the head. The right elbow should point directly toward the right, bent at a right angle. The tip of the sword should be slightly lower than the handle and should be just visible in the peripheral vision of the left eye.

7. Step forward with the right leg, cutting by swinging the sword out and around on a 45° angle with the right hand. Stop the sword with the left hand just in front of the point where the right leg inserts into the hip. The right shoulder and hip should be further forward than the left.

8. Move the handle of the sword out and the tip back until the monouchi rests on the right leg just above the knee. The edge should be perpendicular to the angle of the leg.

9. Switch the grip of the right hand so that the palm faces down.

10. Grasp the scabbard with the left hand, forming a cradle at the opening with the thumb and forefinger.

11. Swing the sword tip around in front of the body and rest the blade on the cradle created by the left hand. The point where the blade contacts the left hand should be about six inches from the tsuba.

12. Slide the sword away from the body at a 45° angle until the tip reaches the opening of the scabbard. Keep it level.

13. Begin to slide the sword into the scabbard while turning the body to bring the shoulders and hip back to square. Begin slowly lowering the body onto the left knee. Both the sliding sword and the dropping motion should begin slowly and gradually decrease in speed. There should be no bump when the knee contacts the ground. Gradually rotate the edge of the blade toward straight up and down while sliding the sword into the scabbard. It should be at an angle of about $10°$ when the sword is fully seated in the scabbard. Let the left hand slide back when it is contacted by the scabbard. As soon as the sword is fully seated, place the thumb of the left hand on the tsuba.

14. Move the right hand to the butt of the handle. Grasp the handle at that point.

15. Stand up by stepping forward with the right leg. The heels should be together, feet pointing outward $45°$. Adjust the sword so that the handle meets the centerline of the body.

16. Move the right hand down to a relaxed position at the side of the body. Step back to the starting point (about three steps), moving the left foot first.

Eight • Pursuit

Hachihon Me • Tsukekomi

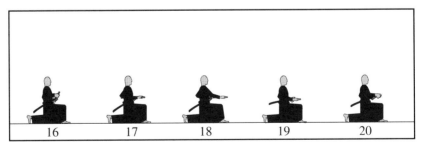

Scenario. From a sitting position, the swordsman prepares to counter an opponent who approaches from the front. When the opponent prepares to attack, the swordsman stands and strikes him on the forehead, then pauses to study the effect. When the swordsman detects an opening, he moves in to finish the opponent, resheathes the sword, then stands up with dignity.

1. Sit in seiza, facing straight ahead.

2. Grasp the scabbard with the left hand. Place the thumb on the tsuba to prevent the sword from slipping.

3. Grasp the handle of the sword, near the tsuba, with the right hand. Move the knees together.

4. Rise onto the knees and onto the balls of the feet.

5. Step out with the right leg. Draw the sword straight ahead, level with the floor. Stop when the first one foot of the sword is out of the scabbard.

6. Movement 6, 7, and 8 are executed in one smooth, continuous motion. Stand up by stepping back with the right foot. Pull the scabbard back with the left hand and use the right hand to raise the sword overhead. Grasp the handle of the sword with the left hand while raising the sword.

7. Step forward with the right foot.

8. Step forward with the left foot to bring the feet together while cutting straight ahead toward an imaginary opponent's forehead. Extend the arms to reach forward with the tip of the blade. Pause momentarily in this position.

9. Raise the sword overhead in a straight line.

10. Step forward with the right foot.

11. Step forward with the left foot to bring the feet together while cutting straight down the centerline.

12. Slide the right foot fully back while raising the blade to *jodan no kamae* (a ready position with the sword held overhead). The right foot should assume a position with the heel turned inward and touching the floor. The elbows should be held wide apart and the handle of the sword should be held above and just in front of the forehead.

13. Rotate the right foot so that the heel moves off the ground while lowering the right knee to the ground. Move the sword forward in a circular path until the butt of the handle is one fist length from the abdomen.

14. Reverse the position of the right hand so that the palm is down.

15. Rotate the sword tip downward until it is in front of the left knee while moving the left hand in front of the knee to receive it. The left hand is held palm open, fingers together and pointing downward at about a 45° angle. The sword should contact the left hand about six inches down from the tsuba.

16. Slide the sword toward the right, pointing the butt slightly toward the right shoulder, at an angle of about 45° above level. Stop when about six inches of the blade remain extended past the left hand.

17. Move the left hand toward the scabbard and the right hand forward and down until the blade is level. Use the right hand to hold the sword in this position while grasping the opening of the scabbard in such a way as to form a cradle for the sword with the thumb and forefinger.

18. Extend the forefinger of the right hand along the side of the handle. Move the sword forward and to the right with the right hand, sliding it on the cradle of the left hand. Pull the scabbard back toward the obi with the left hand at the same time.

19. When the tip of the sword clears the opening of the scabbard, reverse directions and begin to slide the sword into the scabbard. Keep the sword level and on a 45° angle relative to the body. When the tsuba contacts the left hand, let the hand slide back until the sword is fully seated in the scabbard. Move the thumb of the left hand onto the tsuba to keep the sword from slipping.

20. Slide the right hand to the end of the handle and grasp it there.

21. Stand up by stepping forward with the right foot. The heels should be together, feet pointing outward 45°. Adjust the sword so that the handle meets the centerline of the body.

22. Move the right hand down to a relaxed position at the side of the body. Step back to the starting point (about three steps), moving the left foot first.

Nine • Moonbeams

Kyuhon Me • Tsukikage

Scenario. From a sitting position, the swordsman prepares to counter an opponent who approaches from the front. When the opponent draws his sword to attack, the swordsman stands and strikes him across the exposed wrists, then finishes him. He then flips the blade to shake off any blood and resheathes it with dignity.

1. Sit in seiza, facing 45° to the right.

2. Grasp the scabbard with the left hand. Place the thumb on the tsuba to prevent the sword from slipping.

3. Grasp the handle of the sword, near the tsuba, with the right hand. Move the knees together.

4. Rise onto the knees and move onto the balls of the feet, raising the handle of the sword slightly.

5. Shift the weight of the body onto the balls of the feet while turning to face straight ahead. Begin drawing the sword straight ahead, butt of the handle pointing toward an imaginary opponent's forehead.

6. Stand up by stepping forward with the right foot. Draw and strike to temple height, turning the body so that the right shoulder is forward. Pull the scabbard back toward the obi with the left hand.

7. Begin to step forward while bringing the sword overhead. Move the left hand up to grasp the handle.

8. Step fully forward with the left foot.

9. Step fully forward with the right foot.

10. Cut straight down the center, stopping when the butt of the handle is one fist length away from the abdomen.

11. Extend the sword slightly forward without raising or lowering the tip. Rotate the edge about 45° to the right. Open the right hand so that the sword is held between the thumb and the palm of the hand. Move the left hand to press against the scabbard.

12. Extend the sword in a circle moving toward the right. When the arm and sword reach a 45° angle from the body, let the sword swing around toward the rear and bend the right arm at the elbow, bringing the hand straight toward the temple. Stop with the fingers touching the temple.

13. Perform chiburi by whipping the sword in a circle across the front of the body. Step forward with the left during this motion. The left foot should stop about a half foot's length further back than the right. The left heel should be slightly raised. In the standing position, keep the knees bent, the hips low, and the feet pointing out 45°. The right arm should stop slightly in front of the body, with the tip of the sword extended forward and toward the ground.

14. Slide the right foot back until it is about two foot lengths behind the left. The right heel should be pressed downward but not touching the floor. Move the whole sword backwards about one inch while stepping back to compliment the leg motion.

15. Grasp the scabbard in the left hand, making a cradle with the thumb and forefinger which extends past the opening of the scabbard.

16. Move the sword across the front of the body until it rests on the finger cradle at a point on the blade about six inches from the tsuba. The sword should be level, its edge at about a 60° angle below straight up and down.

17. Slide the sword away from the body at a 45° angle until the tip reaches the opening of the scabbard. Keep it level.

18. Begin to slide the sword slowly into the scabbard. Gradually rotate the edge of the blade toward straight up and down while sliding the sword into the scabbard. It should be at an angle of about 10° when the sword is fully seated in the scabbard. Let the left hand slide back when it is contacted by the scabbard. As soon as the sword is fully seated, place the thumb of the left hand on the tsuba.

19. Move the right hand to the butt of the handle. Grasp the handle at that point.

20. Step forward with the right leg. The heels should come together, the feet point outward 45°. Adjust the sword so that the handle meets the centerline of the body.

21. Move the right hand down to a relaxed position at the side of the body. Step back to the starting point (about four steps), moving the left foot first.

Ten • Tailwind

Jippon Me • Oikaze

Scenario. From a standing position, the swordsman prepares to counter an opponent who stands a good distance in front of him. He steps forward and, just as the opponent is about to attack, draws and cuts him across the throat, then finishes him with a downward strike. He then flips the blade to shake off any blood and resheathes the sword with dignity.

1. Stand facing straight ahead, heels together, feet pointing 45° apart. Shoulders should be pulled back and down, arms held relaxed at the sides.

2. Grasp the scabbard with the left hand. Place the thumb on the tsuba to prevent the sword from slipping.

3. Grasp the handle of the sword, near the tsuba, with the right hand.

4. Begin to bend the knees. As the body lowers, allow the weight to shift slightly forward.

5, 6, 7, 8, 9. Slide the feet forward one at a time, right foot first.

10. With the left foot forward, begin to draw the sword straight down center, toward throat level.

11. Step out with the right foot, while drawing the sword into a horizontal cut across the front of the body. Shoulders should be square, arm forward and to the right, and the sword should be level, pointing straight ahead.

12. Begin to step forward while raising the sword overhead.

13. Step forward with the left foot.

14. Step forward with the right foot.

15. Cut straight down center. Step with the butt of the sword handle one fist's length away from the abdomen.

16. Extend the sword slightly forward without raising or lowering the tip. Rotate the edge about 45° to the right. Open the right hand so that the sword is held between the thumb and the palm of the hand. Move the left hand to press against the scabbard.

17. Extend the sword in a circle moving toward the right. When the arm and sword reach a 45° angle from the body, let the sword swing around toward the rear and bend the right arm at the elbow, bringing the hand straight toward the temple. Stop with the fingers touching the temple.

18. Perform chiburi by whipping the sword in a circle across the front of the body. Step forward with the left foot during this motion. The left foot should stop about a half foot's length further back than the right. The left heel should be slightly raised. In the standing position, keep the knees bent, the hips low, and the feet pointing out 45°. The right arm should stop slightly in front of the body, with the tip of the sword extended forward and toward the ground.

19. Slide the right foot back until it is about two foot lengths behind the left. The right heel should be pressed downward but not touching the floor. Move the whole sword backwards about one inch while stepping back to complement the leg motion.

20. Grasp the scabbard in the left hand, making a cradle with the thumb and forefinger which extends past the opening of the scabbard.

21. Move the sword across the front of the body until it rests on the finger cradle at a point on the blade about six inches from the tsuba. The sword should be level, its edge at about a 60° angle below straight up and down.

22. Slide the sword away from the body at a 45° angle until the tip reaches the opening of the scabbard. Keep it level.

23. Begin to slide the sword slowly into the scabbard. Gradually rotate the edge of the blade toward straight up and down while sliding the sword into the scabbard. It should be at an angle of about 10° when the sword is fully seated in the scabbard. Let the left hand slide back when it is contacted by the scabbard. As soon as the sword is fully seated, place the thumb of the left hand on the tsuba.

24. Move the right hand to the butt of the handle. Grasp the handle at that point.

25. Step forward with the right leg. The heels should come together, the feet point outward 45°. Adjust the sword so that the handle meets the centerline of the body.

26. Move the right hand down to a relaxed position at the side of the body. Step back to the starting point (about five steps), moving the left foot first.

Eleven • Sudden Draw

Juippon Me • Nukiuchi

抜打

Scenario. The swordsman sits facing his opponent. Just as the opponent is about to attack, the swordsman draws and finishes him with a downward cut. He then flips the blood off by whipping the sword to the side and resheathes it with dignity.

1. Sit in seiza, facing the shomen.

2. Grasp the scabbard with the left hand. Place the thumb on the tsuba to prevent the sword from slipping.

3. Grasp the handle of the sword, near the tsuba, with the right hand. Rotate the edge of the sword outward about 30° while moving the knees together.

4. Rise onto the knees and move onto the balls of the feet. Begin to draw the sword, with the butt of the handle moving toward the right at throat level.

5. Pull the scabbard back with the left hand to clear the tip of the sword, then raise the sword overhead, keeping the handle to the right of the centerline and the blade angling toward the left to protect from an opponent's strike.

6. Move the left hand up to grasp the handle near the butt.

7. Cut straight down the center, driving forward with the hips for power. The knees may rise slightly off the floor, then drop as the cut is completed. Move the knees apart during the motion to provide a stable base.

8. Perform chiburi by whipping the sword to the side at hip level. The right hand should be forward of the body, the sword level and pointing straight ahead.

9. Move the sword across the front of the body until it rests on the finger cradle at a point on the blade about six inches from the tsuba. The sword should be level, its edge at about a 60° angle below straight up and down.

10. Slide the sword away from the body at a 45° angle until the tip reaches the opening of the scabbard. Keep it level.

11. Begin to slide the sword into the scabbard while slightly lowering the weight of the body. Gradually rotate the edge of the blade toward straight up and down while sliding the sword into the scabbard. It should be at an angle of about 10° when the sword is fully seated in the scabbard. Let the left hand slide back when it is contacted by the scabbard. As soon as the sword is fully seated, place the thumb of the left hand on the tsuba.

12. Move the right hand to the butt of the handle. Grasp the handle at that point. Move the knees together.

13. Lower the body until sitting in seiza.

14. Adjust the sword so that the handle meets the centerline of the body.

15. Move the hands down to rest on the thighs.

Drawing Methods Set

The forms of the Drawing Methods Set (*Batto Ho no Bu*) are as fundamental to standing sword proficiency as those of Seiza no Bu techniques are to learning seiza skills. The first seven forms teach drawing methods which are essential for sword handling. These techniques, although basic, have many advanced applications and can provide material for years of study, making the Batto set as crucial to the beginner as the seiza set.

Batto Ho no Bu also requires that the student learn the correct standing posture. Throughout all of these techniques, the knees must be bent to keep the center of gravity low, the weight must be kept very slightly forward to allow for quick motion, the hips must be tucked and the shoulders pulled down, and the upper body must ride smoothly atop the hips and legs for optimum balance. Hard work to maintain these checkpoints will pay great dividends in a student's later practice, as well as improve physical health.

Batto forms are found in most major sword systems practiced today, with variations according to each system's special characteristics. The forms taught here have details that are specific to Eishin-Ryu, and are named as follows:

1. Ordered Sword One	*Junto Sono Ichi*	84
2. Ordered Sword Two	*Junto Sono Ni*	87
3. Pursuing Sword	*Tsuigekito*	90
4. Angular Sword	*Shato*	93
5. Four Directional Cut One	*Shihoto Sono Ichi*	95
6. Four Directional Cut Two	*Shihoto Sono Ni*	97
7. Beheading Stroke	*Zantotsuto*	99

抜刀法の部

One • Ordered Sword One

Ippon Me • Junto Sono Ichi

順刀其の一

Scenario. The swordsman faces his opponent. As the opponent prepares to attack, the swordsman steps forward, quickly draws and cuts him across the throat, then moves forward to finish him with a downward cut. Flipping the blade to remove any blood, the swordsman resheathes his sword and steps forward in a dignified manner.

1. Stand facing straight toward the shomen. Shoulders should be pulled back and down, hands held relaxed at the sides.

2. Grasp the scabbard with the left hand. Place the thumb on the tsuba to prevent the sword from slipping.

3. Step forward with the right foot.

4. Step forward with the left foot while grasping the handle with the right hand.

5. Begin to draw the sword toward throat level while stepping out with the right foot.

6. Step fully out with the right foot while cutting in a horizontal line across the front of the body.

7, 8. Bring the left foot forward while raising the sword. Be sure to protect the head with the sword while moving it to the overhead position. Move the left hand up to grasp the handle.

9. Step out with the left foot and cut straight down the center.

10. Extend the sword slightly forward without raising or lowering the tip. Rotate the edge about 45° to the right. Open the right hand so that the sword is held between the thumb and the palm of the hand. Move the left hand to press against the scabbard where it intersects the obi.

11. Extend the sword in a circle moving toward the right. When the arm and sword reach a 45° angle from the body, let the sword swing around toward the rear and bend the right arm at the elbow, bringing the hand straight toward the temple. Stop with the fingers touching the temple.

12. Perform chiburi by whipping the sword in a circle across the front of the body. Step forward with the left foot during this motion. The left foot should stop about a half foot's length further back than the right. The left heel should be slightly raised. Keep the knees bent, the hips low, and the feet pointing out 45°. The right arm should end slightly in front of the body, with the tip of the sword extended forward and toward the ground.

13. Slide the left foot back until it is about two foot lengths behind the right. Move the whole sword rearwards about one inch while

85

stepping back to complement the leg motion. The left heel should be pressed downward but not touching the floor.

14. Grasp the scabbard in the left hand, making a cradle with the thumb and forefinger which extends past the opening of the scabbard.

15. Move the sword across the front of the body until it rests on the finger cradle at a point on the blade about six inches from the tsuba. The sword should be level, its edge at about a $60°$ angle below straight up and down.

16. Slide the sword away from the body at a $45°$ angle until the tip reaches the opening of the scabbard. Keep it level.

17. Begin to slide the sword slowly into the scabbard. Gradually rotate the edge of the blade toward straight up and down while sliding the sword into the scabbard. It should be at an angle of about $10°$ when the sword is fully seated in the scabbard. Let the left hand slide back when it is contacted by the scabbard. As soon as the sword is fully seated, place the thumb of the left hand on the tsuba.

18. Move the right hand to the butt of the handle. Grasp the handle at that point.

19. Step forward with the left leg. The heels should come together, with the feet pointing outward $45°$. Adjust the sword so that the handle meets the centerline of the body.

20. Move the right hand down to a relaxed position at the side of the body. Step back to the starting point (about five steps), moving the left foot first.

Two • Ordered Sword Two
Nihon Me • Junto Sono Ni

順刀其の二

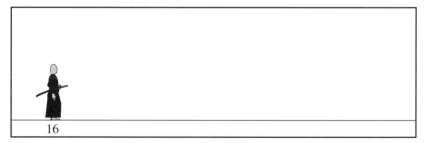

Scenario. The swordsman faces his opponent. As the opponent prepares to attack, the swordsman steps forward, quickly draws and cuts the opponent across the throat, then moves forward to finish him with a downward cut. Flipping the blade to remove any blood, the swordsman resheathes his sword and steps forward in a dignified manner.

1. Stand facing the shomen. Shoulders should be pulled back and down, hands held relaxed at the sides.

2. Grasp the scabbard with the left hand. Place the thumb on the tsuba to prevent the sword from slipping.

3. Step forward with the right foot.

4. Step forward with the left foot while grasping the handle with the right hand.

5. Begin to draw the sword toward throat level while stepping out with the right foot.

6. Step fully out with the right foot while cutting in a horizontal line across the front of the body.

7, 8. Bring the left foot forward while raising the sword. Be sure to protect the head with the sword while moving it to the overhead position. Move the left hand up to grasp the handle.

9. Step out with the right foot and cut straight down the center.

10. Perform chiburi by whipping the sword to the side at hip level. The right hand should be forward of the body, the sword level and pointing straight ahead. Move the left hand back to press against the scabbard.

11. Grasp the scabbard with the left hand, forming a cradle at the opening with the thumb and forefinger. Move the sword across the front of the body until it rests on the finger cradle at a point on the blade about six inches from the tsuba. The sword should be level, its edge at about a 60° angle below straight up and down.

12. Slide the sword away from the body at a 45° angle until the tip reaches the opening of the scabbard. Keep it level.

13. Begin to slide the sword into the scabbard. Gradually rotate the edge of the blade toward straight up and down while sliding the sword into the scabbard. It should be at an angle of about 10° when the sword is fully seated in the scabbard. Let the left hand slide back

when it is contacted by the scabbard. As soon as the sword is fully seated, place the thumb of the left hand on the tsuba.

14. Move the right hand to the butt of the handle. Grasp the handle at that point.

15. Step forward with the left foot.

16. Adjust the sword so that the handle meets the centerline of the body. Move the right hand down to the side of the body. Step back to the starting position, left foot first.

Three • Pursuing Sword

Sanbon Me • Tsuigekito

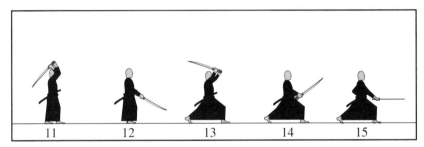

Scenario. The swordsman faces his opponent. As the opponent prepares to draw his sword, the swordsman steps forward, quickly draws and prevents him from drawing by cutting at his wrist, then moves forward to stun him with a cut to the forehead. Pausing a moment to study the effect of his actions, the swordsman sees an opening and moves in to finish his opponent with a downward cut. Flipping the blade to remove any blood, the swordsman resheathes his sword and steps forward in a dignified manner.

1. Stand facing the shomen. Shoulders should be pulled back and down, hands held relaxed at the sides.

2. Grasp the scabbard with the left hand. Place the thumb on the tsuba to prevent the sword from slipping.

3. Step forward with the right foot.

4. Take a half step forward with the left foot while grasping the handle with the right hand.

5. Begin to draw the sword toward the right shoulder of an imaginary opponent while stepping out with the right foot.

6. Step fully out with the right foot while drawing the sword at an angle that takes the tip on a path from opponent's right shoulder toward the left hip, stopping at a position where the opponent's wrist would be if he were drawing his own sword. Pull the scabbard backward with the left hand.

7. Step forward with the left foot while bringing the sword overhead. Move the left hand up to grasp the handle.

8, 9. Step forward with the right foot and then bring the left foot forward to match it while striking straight ahead to forehead height. Pause for a moment in this position.

10. Raise the sword to the overhead position.

11, 12. Step forward with the right foot and then bring the left foot forward to match it while cutting straight down center.

13. Slide the right foot back while raising the sword to jodan no kamae.

14. Step all the way back with the left foot while lowering the sword to chudan no kamae.

15–21. Perform chiburi and finish as in Ordered Sword Two (p. 87). Step back to the starting position, left foot first.

Four • Angular Sword
Yonhon Me • Shato

Scenario. The swordsman faces his opponent. As the opponent draws his sword, the swordsman steps forward, quickly draws and prevents him from cutting by striking at his raised forearms, then moves forward while cutting him with a diagonal stroke. The swordsman then moves to the right (to avoid being cut) and cuts again, this time to a lower point on his opponent's body. Flipping the blade to remove any blood, the swordsman resheathes his sword and steps forward in a dignified manner.

1. Stand facing the shomen. Shoulders should be pulled back and down, hands held relaxed at the sides.

2. Grasp the scabbard with the left hand. Place the thumb on the tsuba to prevent the sword from slipping.

3. Step forward with the right foot.

4. Take a half step forward with the left foot while grasping the handle with the right hand.

5. Begin to draw the sword toward the right shoulder of an imaginary opponent while stepping out with the right foot.

6. Step fully out with the right foot while drawing the sword on an angle that takes the tip forward and upward toward the opponent's temple. Pull the scabbard backward with the left hand.

7. Bring the left foot forward while raising the sword overhead. Move the left hand up to grasp the handle.

8. Step out with the left foot while cutting on a *kesa* angle (from opponent's right shoulder to opposite hip).

9. Step toward the right front with the right foot while raising the sword overhead. Pivot the body to face the left front.

10. Slide the left foot toward the right rear while cutting on the reverse kesa angle (from the opponent's left shoulder to right hip). The right shoulder will end up slightly forward of the left.

11. Move the right shoulder back so that the body is squared toward the left front while bringing the sword to chudan no kamae.

12–18. Perform chiburi and finish as in Ordered Sword Two (p. 87). Step back to the starting position after aligning the body to face in the direction of the shomen, moving the left foot first.

Five • Four Directional Cut One

Gohon Me • Shihoto Sono Ichi

四方刀其の一

Scenario. The swordsman is surrounded by four opponents, one at his left rear, one each at his left and right front, and one directly ahead. Taking an opportunity to go on the offensive, the swordsman draws and thrusts his sword into the opponent at the left rear corner, then turns and cuts down the one at the right front. Turning to the left front and directly ahead, he dispatches those opponents in their respective places. Flipping the blade to remove any blood, the swordsman re-sheathes his sword and steps forward in a dignified manner.

1. Stand facing the shomen. Shoulders should be pulled back and down, hands held relaxed at the sides.

2. Grasp the scabbard with the left hand. Place the thumb on the tsuba to prevent the sword from slipping.

3. Step forward with the right foot.

4. Step forward with the left foot while grasping the handle with the right hand.

5. Step out toward the front right while preparing to draw the sword on the same angle, parallel to the floor. Rotate the sword and scabbard outward until the blade is flat (parallel to the floor).

6. Draw the sword until only the tip remains inside the scabbard.

7. Look back toward the left rear corner. Pull the scabbard back with the left hand until it is perpendicular to the path made by the sword, clearing the sword tip. Thrust the sword back toward the left rear corner, stopping with the tsuba touching the left pectoral area.

8. Turn to face the right front corner and raise the sword overhead. Move the left hand up to grasp the handle.

9. Cut straight down toward the right front corner.

10. Step all the way across to the left front corner with the right foot while raising the sword overhead.

11. Cut straight down toward the left front corner.

12. Step directly toward the front with the right foot while raising the sword overhead.

13. Cut straight down the center.

14–20. Perform chiburi and finish as in Ordered Sword Two (p. 87). Step back to the starting position, moving the left foot first.

Six • Four Directional Cut Two

Roppon Me • Shihoto Sono Ni

四
方
刀
其
の
二

Scenario. The swordsman is surrounded by four opponents, one at his left rear, one each at his left and right front, and one directly ahead. Taking an opportunity to go on the offensive, the swordsman draws and thrusts the sword into the opponent at the left rear corner, then turns and cuts down the one at the right front. Turning to the left front and directly ahead, he dispatches the opponents in their respective places. Flipping the blade to remove any blood, the swordsman resheathes his sword and steps forward in a dignified manner.

97

1. Stand facing the shomen. Shoulders should be pulled back and down, hands held relaxed at the sides.

2. Grasp the scabbard with the left hand. Place the thumb on the tsuba to prevent the sword from slipping.

3. Step forward with the right foot.

4. Step forward with the left foot while grasping the handle with the right hand.

5. Step out toward front right while preparing to draw the sword on the same angle, parallel to the floor. Rotate the sword and scabbard outward until the blade is flat (parallel to the floor).

6. Draw the sword until only the tip remains inside the scabbard.

7. Look back toward the left rear corner. Pull the scabbard back with the left hand until it is perpendicular to the path made by the sword, clearing the sword tip. Thrust the sword back toward the left rear corner, stopping with the tsuba touching the left pectoral area.

8. Turn to face the right front corner and raise the sword overhead. Move the left hand up to grasp the handle.

9. Cut straight down toward the right front corner.

10. Step all the way forward to the left front corner with the left foot while raising the sword overhead.

11. Cut straight down toward the left front corner.

12. Step directly toward the front with the right foot while raising the sword overhead.

13. Cut straight down center.

14–20. Perform chiburi and finish as in Ordered Sword Two (p. 87). Step back to the starting position, moving the left foot first.

Seven • Beheading Stroke

Nanahon Me • Zantotsuto

斬
突
刀

Scenario. The swordsman faces his opponent. As the opponent prepares to draw his sword, the swordsman steps forward, quickly draws and prevents him from drawing by cutting at his wrist. Then, pressing down with his sword to continue to control his opponent's sword, he slides forward, cutting his chest, and finally moves in to finish him with a downward cut. Flipping the blade to remove any blood, the swordsman resheathes his sword and steps forward in a dignified manner.

1. Stand facing the shomen. Shoulders should be pulled back and down, hands held relaxed at the sides.

2. Grasp the scabbard with the left hand. Place the thumb on the tsuba to prevent the sword from slipping.

3. Step forward with the right foot.

4. Take a half step forward with the left foot while grasping the handle with the right hand.

5. Begin to draw the sword toward the right shoulder of an imaginary opponent while stepping out with the right foot.

6. Step fully out with the right foot while drawing the sword on an angle that takes the tip on a path from opponent's right shoulder toward the left hip, stopping at a position where the opponent's wrist would be if he were drawing his own sword. Pull the scabbard backward with the left hand.

7. Step forward with the left foot while moving the sword to *chudan no kamae* (a position with the arms extended so that the butt of the sword is one fist width away from the abdomen and the tip is held up at throat level).

8. Step out with the right left, thrusting forward with the sword. Keep the tip slightly higher than the handle throughout this motion.

9. Step forward with the left foot, again moving the sword to chudan no kamae.

10. Raise the sword overhead.

11. Step out with the right foot. Cut straight down center.

12–18. Perform chiburi and finish as in Ordered Sword Two (p. 87). Step back to the starting position, moving the left foot first.

The Intermediate
and Advanced
Practitioner

⬤ Intermediate and Advanced Practice

After a period of iaido practice, from perhaps two to five years depending on the frequency and dedication of training, general coordination, past experience in martial arts and quality of instruction, the iaido practitioner should begin to demonstrate a deeper understanding of the movements that make up the beginning techniques. There should come a smoothness which shows that the iaidoka is no longer thinking ahead to the next move while demonstrating but, instead, is concentrating on more general issues of correct form, rhythm, and strength in movement. There are several points on which such intermediate students should concentrate.

One such point is eliminating excess sword and body motions. Iaido is an art form and is designed to affect the character of the individual practicing it. Eliminating impurities in the form ties directly into the process of refining the character, so it is of utmost importance that the student concentrate on this aspect of training.

The usual point at which excess motions appear is in and around the major cut in each form. These motions commonly take two forms: in one, the student will raise the sword overhead and then further cock the sword just before making the cut. This is unacceptable, strategically and artistically. From a strategic point of view, the delay and telegraphing of intent that this motion causes would lead to weakness. From an artistic point of view, any deviation from the ideal diminishes the beauty of the form, and the ideal cut is fast and strong and appears almost out of nowhere. Signs of effort are to be avoided.

The second common flaw comes at the end of the cut. Beginning iaidoka often let their bodies dip forward at the end of the cut. Similarly, to decrease the momentum of the cut, they often allow the sword to bob or quiver at the finishing point of the cutting stroke. These weaknesses must be eliminated, and the only way known to eliminate them is through hard, concentrated practice. While training, the student must concentrate on the four points of kirioroshi listed earlier in this book.

Another impurity which relates directly to the martial value of iaido practice is the angle at which the blade is held. In order for the sword to cut properly, the blade must be held at the same angle as the cut that is being made. In other words, for a straight cut, the blade must be held perfectly straight and, for an angular cut, the blade angle must match the angle at which the sword moves through the air. If these angles are different, then the sword would twist or break if it were actually used to cut. Since most students of iaido do not practice actual cutting, weakness in this area is widespread. To eliminate the weakness, the student must concentrate on the blade angle during practice, perhaps slowing down the cutting motions and examining the path taken by the blade to determine whether or not the blade angle matches the cutting path. Many of the better iaido practice swords are designed to produce a swishing sound during the cut, and most of these produce the loudest sound when the blade is held at the optimum angle, which can be a useful guide for the student.

Other typical points of form, besides an upright posture and and correct angles for each body part, involve the speed at which motions are executed. There are moves with two types of moving checkpoints in iaido. The first are those which are meant to start out slowly and gradually speed up, so that they are fastest just before the end of the motion. All drawing motions fall into this group.

The other type of moves are those that are meant to start out slowly and get slower. Dropping onto one knee, replacing the sword in the scabbard, and various other special moves should be done this way. The speeding-up motions should accelerate smoothly throughout their path and should stop cleanly, without any signs of effort. The motions which decelerate should do so gradually, and the iaidoka should use the opportunity to demonstrate *zanshin*, which will be discussed in more detail in the next section.

The most important aspect to remember is that budo is an expression of the character of its participants. The student who desires to excel in iaido must practice wholeheartedly, putting aside thoughts of quickly gaining more rank or learning many techniques. The practice, for the most part, must be done for its own sake, because the student enjoys it. It is very unusual for someone who doesn't care for hard practice to excel, especially in this art of refinement and dry precision. The only way to become proficient at iaido is to practice hard over a long period of time, examining the techniques carefully to reach an understanding of their purpose and how to best perform them, and examining oneself carefully to gradually try to remove the negative motivations for practicing and to replace them with love for the art, a desire to improve, and an attitude of respect for the teachers and other forebears of the art.

The Samurai Sitting Method

According to information available about feudal Japan, the samurai often found it too cumbersome to rise quickly from the seiza position, so they modified it to suit their need for readiness. The new stance is called *tatehiza* ("raised knee") and looks like seiza except that the right leg is placed in front of the body, with the knee, of course, raised. From this position, it is much easier to shift the weight of the body onto the front leg and move into a one knee up kneeling position, or to stand. The tatehiza position forms the basis for two major sets of forms, Seated Set *(Tatehiza no Bu)* and the advanced set, Secret Forms, Seated Set *(Okuiai Iwaza no Bu)*.

To sit in the tatehiza position, stand and place the left foot about twenty centimeters behind the right foot. Sit by bending the knees and placing left leg down, with the ball of the foot and the knee touching the floor. Reach down with the right hand and lightly slap the hakama out to the left so that it doesn't bunch up under the leg. Move the left foot so that it is flat on the floor, slap the hakama out from under the right leg, then sit down on the left leg. Pull the right leg in toward the body until the toes are just forward of the left knee. Place the right hand atop the right knee, and the left hand near the hip on the left side of the body as shown in the figures 1 and 2. The back should be straight, eyes looking four meters ahead.

Students of iaido generally find this sitting posture uncomfortable for the first few months of practice. It is difficult to balance in, and the left leg often becomes rather painful. With regular practice, though, it should become comfortable.

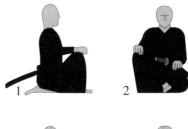

1

2

3

4

Figures 3 and 4 show the position which ends most tatehiza forms. From a standard kneeling position with one knee up, the right leg (usually) is slid straight back, then out to the right. The left leg is then pivoted on the knee to bring the left foot next to the right. To stand, slide the right foot forward on a diagonal path toward center, back to the kneeling position, and stand by stepping forward with the left foot.

Eye Contact, Focus, and Dignity

Metsuke means "eye contact." In iaido, it refers to the position of the eyes during a technique. In order to simulate real interaction between swordsmen, the eyes must be fixed on a position where the opponent might be standing. To accomplish this, train the eyes on a point four meters (about twelve feet) ahead at the beginning of a technique, as in figure 1, and keep them there up until the moment of the cut. Simultaneously with the cut, drop the eyes to a point three meters (about nine feet) ahead, as in figure 2. They should remain fixed on this closer point until the end of the technique. At the finish, the eyes move up to look straight ahead when the sheathed sword is moved back to a position in front of the center of the body.

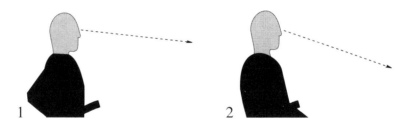

1   2

This method of fixing the eyes is part of the overall concentration a student should bring to practice, which includes technique, mental focus, and spiritual intent. All of these elements should be focused throughout the execution of a technique. The Japanese word for this kind of focus is *kiai*, a compound made up of the word *ki*, intrinsic energy, and the word *ai*, meaning "to bring together," or "to focus." The word is commonly used to refer to the shout often heard during martial arts practice. This shout is simply an outward manifestation of the concentrated energy of the practitioner, but whether or not an actual shout is heard, kiai should always be present during the practice of martial arts.

Zanshin means "reserved spirit," and refers to the dignity and power of the advanced martial artist. Such a person seems to radiate a kind of quiet power, suggesting a greater spiritual power beneath the surface. This is the kind of poise that one should strive to acquire in iaido practice, and it should be especially noticable at the beginning of a technique, before any movements are made, and at the end, when the focused energy shown during the technique seems to linger. The intermediate and advanced students of iaido should practice pausing for one or two seconds after major motions in a technique while continuing to focus concentration. In time, the quality of zanshin will begin to develop.

Intermediate
Techniques

Secret Forms, Drawing Methods Set

T hese four forms are part of the Drawing Methods Set (*Batto Ho no Bu*) introduced earlier, but are usually taught at the intermediate level, since they are considered secret techniques (*oku no waza*). They are the introduction to three important facets of swordsmanship: drawing from a natural walking motion; rising draws and cuts; and the fast method of *noto* (resheathing the sword). The walking method comes from the swordsman's need to defend against opponents who are surrounding him, usually multiple opponents and usually on both sides or around him. The rising draw, which is actually a cut, is one of the fastest methods of turning the draw into an effective attack. The fast noto, while not necessarily related to sword defense or attack skills, demands a high level of control since the hardness of the sword's cutting edges can quickly wear through the soft wood of the scabbard. The student should strive to perfect his noto; it should be a quick, efficient motion that is almost silent and that barely brings the sword into contact with the sides of the scabbard. The names of the forms are as follows:

1. Forward Inverse Cut	*Zenteki Gyaku To*	114
2. Multi-Directional Cut	*Tateki To*	117
3. Rearward Inverse Cut	*Koteki Gyaku To*	120
4. Rearward Quick Draw	*Koteki Nukiuchi*	123

抜刀法の部

前敵逆刀

One • Forward Inverse Cut
Ippon Me • Zenteki Gyaku To

Scenario. A swordsman and his opponent begin to move toward one another. Just as his opponent draws his sword and raises it overhead, the swordsman draws in an upward arc, cutting his opponent along the front of his body. The swordsman then steps forward and finishes his opponent with a downward cut, flips the blood off his sword and resheathes it with dignity.

1. Stand facing the shomen. Shoulders should be pulled back and down, hands held relaxed at the sides.

2. Step forward with the right foot. Let the left arm swing forward.

3. Step forward with the left foot, letting the right arm swing forward.

4. Step forward with the right foot while grasping the scabbard with the left hand.

5. Step forward with the left foot. Grasp the handle of the sword with the right hand.

6. Begin to draw the sword, keeping it level with the ground.

7. Take a large step forward with the right foot while continuing to draw the sword. When the tip nears the opening of the scabbard, rotate both sword and scabbard until the edge faces downward. Draw the sword on a rising angle across the front of the body, from the lower left side moving toward the upper right. At the end of the cut, the sword should be above and to the right of the head, parallel to the floor, pointing straight ahead with the edge up. The left heel is down.

8. Step forward with the left foot while raising the sword overhead. Move the left hand up to grasp the handle.

9. Cut on the kesa angle (upper right to lower left) while stepping out with the right foot. The body should turn slightly so that the right hip and shoulder end up forward of the left. The left heel is down.

10. Turn the body to face straight ahead while raising the sword to chudan position. The left heel comes up off the ground.

11. Perform chiburi by whipping the sword to the side at hip level. The right hand should be forward of the body, the sword level and pointing straight ahead. Move the left hand back to press against the scabbard.

12. Grasp the scabbard with the left hand, forming a cradle at the opening with the thumb and forefinger. Move the sword across the front of the body until it rests on the finger cradle at a point on the blade about six inches from the tsuba. The sword should be level, its edge at about a 60° angle below straight up and down.

13. Slide the sword away from the body at a 45° angle until the tip reaches the opening of the scabbard. Keep it level.

14. Begin to slide the sword into the scabbard. Once the tip is inside the scabbard, move the first two-thirds of the blade into the scabbard in one quick motion. Finish moving the sword inward very slowly. Let the left hand slide back when it is contacted by the scabbard. As soon as the sword is fully seated, place the thumb of the left hand on the tsuba.

15. Step forward with the left foot.

16. Move the right hand to the butt of the handle and grasp it there. Adjust the sword so that the handle meets the centerline of the body. Step back to the starting position, moving the left foot first. At the starting position, move the right hand down to a relaxed position at the side of the body.

Two • Multi-Directional Cut

Batto Ho no Oku • Tateki To

Scenario. A swordsman, surrounded by three opponents, detects a strategic opening. He draws his sword and thrusts it backward into one opponent, turns to the right front and finishes another with a downward cut, then turns to the left front and finishes the third opponent. Finally, he flips the blood off the sword and resheathes it with dignity.

1. Stand facing the shomen. Shoulders should be pulled back and down, hands held relaxed at the sides.

2. Step forward with the right foot. Let the left arm swing forward.

3. Step forward with the left foot, letting the right arm swing forward.

4. Step forward with the right foot while grasping the scabbard with the left hand.

5. Step forward with the left foot. Grasp the handle of the sword with the right hand.

6. Step out toward the front right while preparing to draw the sword on the same angle, parallel to the floor. Rotate the sword and scabbard outward until the blade is flat (parallel to the floor).

7. Draw the sword until only the tip remains inside the scabbard.

8. Look back toward the left rear corner. Pull the scabbard back with the left hand until it is perpendicular to the path made by the sword, clearing the sword tip. Thrust the sword back toward the left rear corner, stopping with the tsuba touching the left pectoral area.

9. Turn to face the right front corner and raise the sword overhead. Move the left hand up to grasp the handle.

10. Cut straight down toward the right front corner.

11. Step across to the left front corner with the left foot while raising the sword overhead.

12. Cut straight down toward the left front corner.

13. Perform chiburi by whipping the sword to the side at hip level. The right hand should be forward of the body, the sword level and pointing straight ahead. Move the left hand back to press against the scabbard.

14. Grasp the scabbard with the left hand, forming a cradle at the opening with the thumb and forefinger. Move the sword across the

front of the body until it rests on the finger cradle at a point on the blade about six inches from the tsuba. The sword should be level, its edge at about a 60° angle below straight up and down.

15. Slide the sword away from the body at a 45° angle until the tip reaches the opening of the scabbard. Keep it level.

16. Begin to slide the sword into the scabbard. Once the tip is inside the scabbard, move the first two-thirds of the blade into the scabbard in one quick motion. Finish moving the sword inward very slowly. Let the left hand slide back when it is contacted by the scabbard. As soon as the sword is fully seated, place the thumb of the left hand on the tsuba.

17. Step forward with the right foot.

18. Move the right hand to the butt of the handle and grasp it there. Adjust the sword so that the handle meets the centerline of the body. Step back to the starting position moving the left foot first to return the body to a forward-facing position. At the starting position, move the right hand down to a relaxed position at the side of the body.

Three • Rearward Inverse Cut

Sanbon Me • Koteki Gyaku To

後敵逆刀

Scenario. A swordsman, between two opponents, detects a strategic opening. He turns to his rear, draws his sword and cuts along the front of the opponent's body there, then turns back toward the front and finishes that opponent with an angular downward cut. Finally, he flips the blood off the sword and resheaths it with dignity.

1. Stand facing the shomen. Shoulders should be pulled back and down, hands held relaxed at the sides.

2. Step forward with the right foot. Let the left arm swing forward.

3. Step forward with the left foot, letting the right arm swing forward.

4. Step forward with the right foot while grasping the scabbard with the left hand.

5. Step forward with the left foot. Grasp the handle of the sword with the right hand.

6. Step forward with the right foot.

7. Pivot toward the rear, turning by pivoting on the right heel, then the left. Begin to draw the sword parallel with the floor while turning.

8. When the tip nears the opening of the scabbard, rotate both sword and scabbard until the edge faces downward. Draw the sword on a rising angle across the front of the body, from the lower left side toward the upper right. At the end of the cut, the sword should be above and to the right of the head, parallel to the floor, pointing straight ahead with the edge up. Step forward with the left foot. The right heel is down. The left hand presses against the scabbard.

9. Pivot toward the front, turning by pivoting on the left heel, then the right. Raise the sword overhead while turning. Move the left hand up to grasp the handle.

10. Cut on the kesa angle (upper right to lower left) while stepping out with the right foot. The body should turn slightly so that the right hip and shoulder end up forward of the left. The left heel is down.

11. Turn the body to face straight ahead while raising the sword to chudan position. The left heel comes up off the ground.

12. Perform chiburi by whipping the sword to the side at hip level. The right hand should be forward of the body, the sword level and pointing straight ahead. Move the left hand back to press against the scabbard.

13. Grasp the scabbard with the left hand, forming a cradle at the opening with the thumb and forefinger. Move the sword across the front of the body until it rests on the finger cradle at a point on the blade about six inches from the tsuba. The sword should be level, its edge at about a 60° angle below straight up and down.

14. Slide the sword away from the body at a 45° angle until the tip reaches the opening of the scabbard. Keep it level.

15. Begin to slide the sword into the scabbard. Once the tip is inside the scabbard, move the first two-thirds of the blade into the scabbard in one quick motion. Finish moving the sword inward very slowly. Let the left hand slide back when it is contacted by the scabbard. As soon as the sword is fully seated, place the thumb of the left hand on the tsuba.

16. Step forward with the left foot.

17. Move the right hand to the butt of the handle and grasp it there. Adjust the sword so that the handle meets the centerline of the body. Step back to the starting position moving the left foot first. At the starting position, move the right hand down to a relaxed position at the side of the body.

Four • Rearward Quick Draw
Yonhon Me • Koteki Nukiuchi

後敵抜打

Scenario. A swordsman, between two opponents, detects a strategic opening. He turns to his rear, draws his sword and cuts downward along the front of the opponent's body there, then turns back toward the front and finishes that opponent with an angular downward cut. Finally, he flips the blood off the sword and resheathes it with dignity.

1. Stand facing the shomen. Shoulders should be pulled back and down, hands held relaxed at the sides.

2. Step forward with the right foot. Let the left arm swing forward.

3. Step forward with the left foot, letting the right arm swing forward.

4. Step forward with the right foot while grasping the scabbard with the left hand.

5. Step forward with the left foot. Grasp the handle of the sword with the right hand.

6. Pivot toward the rear, turning by pivoting on the left heel, then the right. Begin to draw the sword in an upward direction while turning. Pull the scabbard back with the left hand.

7. When the sword tip clears the scabbard, whip it around in an arc in front of the body to stop at a point just beyond the right foot.

8. Pivot toward the front, turning by pivoting on the right heel, then the lelft. Raise the sword overhead while turning. Move the left hand up to grasp the handle.

9. Cut on the kesa angle (upper left to lower right) while stepping out with the left foot. The body should turn slightly so that the left hip and shoulder end up forward of the left. The right heel is down.

10. Turn the body to face straight ahead while raising the sword to chudan position. The right heel comes up off the ground.

11. Perform chiburi by whipping the sword to the side at hip level. The right hand should be forward of the body, the sword level and pointing straight ahead. Move the left hand back to press against the scabbard.

12. Grasp the scabbard with the left hand, forming a cradle at the opening with the thumb and forefinger. Move the sword across the front of the body until it rests on the finger cradle at a point on the blade about six inches from the tsuba. The sword should be level, its edge at about a $60°$ angle below straight up and down.

13. Slide the sword away from the body at a 45° angle until the tip reaches the opening of the scabbard. Keep it level.

14. Begin to slide the sword into the scabbard. Once the tip is inside the scabbard, move the first two-thirds of the blade into the scabbard in one quick motion. Finish moving the sword inward very slowly. Let the left hand slide back when it is contacted by the scabbard. As soon as the sword is fully seated, place the thumb of the left hand on the tsuba.

15. Step forward with the right foot.

16. Move the right hand to the butt of the handle and grasp it there. Adjust the sword so that the handle meets the centerline of the body. Step back to the starting position moving the left foot first. At the starting position, move the right hand down to a relaxed position at the side of the body.

Half-Seated Set

T he techniques of the Half-Seated Set (*Tatehiza no Bu*) include some of the most challenging in Eishin-Ryu. The half-seated position, though convenient for a quick transition into a strategically useful stance, is extremely difficult for Westerners to master. The deep bends in the knees and the balance throughout the kneeling positions are awkward for our relatively long legs, unaccustomed to sitting on the floor as we are. Nothing else, however, will develop the leg muscles as well or provide such an efficient means of rising to meet an opponent.

In practicing *tatehiza* forms, pay particular attention to the position of the upper body. It should rise straight from the hips, without any extra bobbing or weaving motions, and the head should remain in an alert, upright position. The leg motions should be done smoothly and deliberately. Once the initial problems with balance are worked out, there should be no sudden steps. Each motion procedes only after the previous motion is finished, and each should be precise and complete. The body parts most essential to good tatehiza practice are the hips. All balance in these forms depends on the hips, and they provide the means of transferring power from the legs to the upper body. The names of the forms are as follows:

1.	Cloud Bank	*Yokogumo*	127
2.	Tiger's Step	*Toraisoku*	130
3.	Lightning	*Inazuma*	133
4.	Floating Clouds	*Ukigumo*	136
5.	Mountain Wind	*Oroshi*	139
6.	Breaking Waves	*Iwanami*	142
7.	Fish Scaling	*Urokogaeshi*	145
8.	Returning Waves	*Namigaeshi*	148
9.	Waterfall	*Takiotoshi*	151
10.	Facing Front	*Makkoh*	154

One • Cloud Bank

Ippon Me • Yokogumo

横雲

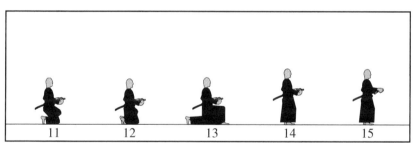

Scenario. A swordsman faces an opponent. Both are seated. As the opponent prepares to attack, the swordsman quickly draws and cuts him across the throat, then finishes him with a downward cut. Flipping the blade to remove any blood, the swordsman resheathes his sword and stands up in a dignified manner.

1. Sit facing the shomen, left leg tucked under the body and right foot tucked near the left knee. The right knee should be up, so that the leg makes a 45° angle upward toward the right. The left fist rests near the hip joint of the left leg; the right fist rests atop the right knee.

2. Grasp the handle of the sword with the right hand, the scabbard with the left, and rotate them outward slightly while moving the left knee inward.

127

3. Rise onto the left knee while beginning to draw the sword toward throat level.

4. Step out with the right foot and draw straight across the front of the body, stopping when the arm extends 45° to the right. The sword should be level and should point straight ahead. Pull the scabbard back with the left hand.

5. Begin to raise the sword overhead while sliding the right foot slightly forward.

6. Move the left hand up to grasp the handle.

7. Cut straight down the center while pulling in with the right foot.

8. Perform chiburi by whipping the sword to the right at hip level. The sword should stop in a position pointing straight ahead and level with the ground. The tsuba should be even with the right knee, about fifteen centimeters to its right. Move the left hand back to press against the scabbard.

9. Grasp the scabbard with the left hand, forming a cradle at the opening with the thumb and forefinger. Move the sword across the front of the body until it rests on the finger cradle at a point on the blade about six inches from the tsuba. The sword should be level, its edge at about a 60° angle below straight up and down.

10. Slide the sword away from the body at a 45° angle until the tip reaches the opening of the scabbard. Keep it level.

11. Begin to slide the sword into the scabbard. At the same time, slide the right foot back until it is even with the left foot, then slide it out to the right about ten inches. The right knee should move back and out.

12. When the right foot is set, move the left foot inward by pivoting on the knee. The inside edges of the feet should be touching. Let the left hand slide back when it is contacted by the scabbard. As soon as the sword is fully seated, place the thumb of the left hand on the tsuba.

13. Slide the right foot forward on a diagonal path until the right leg forms a right angle. Weight is still on the left knee.

14. Stand up by stepping forward with the left foot.

15. Move the right hand to the butt of the handle and grasp it there. Adjust the sword so that the handle meets the centerline of the body. Step back to the starting position moving the left foot first. At the starting position, move the right hand down to a relaxed position at the side of the body.

Two • Tiger's Step
Nihon Me • Toraisoku

虎
一
足

Scenario. A swordsman faces an opponent. Both are seated. As the opponent prepares to attack with a low strike, the swordsman quickly draws and parries the strike, then finishes him with a downward cut. Flipping the blade to remove any blood, the swordsman resheathes his sword and stands up in a dignified manner.

1. Sit facing the shomen, left left tucked under the body and right foot tucked near the left knee. The right knee should be up, so that the

leg makes a 45° angle upward toward the right. The left fist rests near the hip joint of the left leg; the right fist rests atop the right knee.

2. Grasp the handle of the sword with the right hand, the scabbard with the left, and rotate the sword outward slightly while moving the left knee inward.

3. Begin to rise onto the balls of both feet.

4. Continue to rise while drawing the sword straight ahead, level with the floor.

5. As soon as the sword tip clears the scabbard, step back with the left foot and drive downwards and sideways with the flat of the sword.

6. Move the left knee forward and down until it rests near the right foot. Begin to raise the sword overhead.

7. Move the left hand up to grasp the handle. Slide the right foot forward.

8. Cut straight down the center while pulling in with the right foot.

9. Perform chiburi by whipping the sword to the right at hip level. The sword should stop in a position pointing straight ahead and level with the ground. The tsuba should be even with the right knee, about fifteen centimeters to its right. Move the left hand back to press against the scabbard.

10. Grasp the scabbard with the left hand, forming a cradle at the opening with the thumb and forefinger. Move the sword across the front of the body until it rests on the finger cradle at a point on the blade about six inches from the tsuba. The sword should be level, its edge at about a 60° angle below straight up and down.

11. Slide the sword away from the body at a 45° angle until the tip reaches the opening of the scabbard. Keep it level.

12. Begin to slide the sword into the scabbard. At the same time, slide the right foot back until it is even with the left, then slide it out to the right about ten inches. The right knee moves back and out.

13. When the right foot is set, move the left foot inward by pivoting on the knee. The inside edges of the feet should be touching. Let the left hand slide back when it is contacted by the scabbard. As soon as the sword is fully seated, place the thumb of the left hand on the tsuba.

14. Slide the right foot forward on a diagonal path until the right leg forms a right angle. Weight is still on the left knee.

15. Stand up by stepping forward with the left foot.

16. Move the right hand to the butt of the handle and grasp it there. Adjust the sword so that the handle meets the centerline of the body. Step back to the starting position moving the left foot first. At the starting position, move the right hand down to a relaxed position at the side of the body.

Three • Lightning

Sanbon Me • Inazuma

稲妻

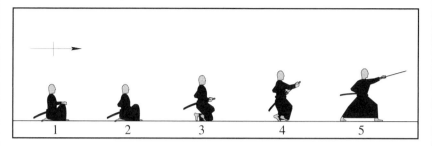

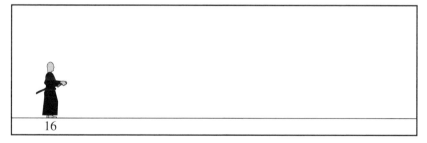

Scenario. A swordsman faces an opponent. Both are seated. As the opponent prepares to attack with a low strike, the swordsman quickly draws and parries the strike, then finishes him with a downward cut. Flipping the blade to remove any blood, the swordsman resheathes his sword and stands up in a dignified manner.

1. Sit facing the shomen, left left tucked under the body and right foot tucked near the left knee. The right knee should be up, so that the

133

that the leg makes a 45° angle upward toward the right. The left fist rests near the hip joint of the left leg; the right fist rests atop the right knee.

2. Grasp the handle of the sword with the right hand, the scabbard with the left, and rotate the sword outward slightly while moving the left knee inward.

3. Begin to rise onto the balls of both feet.

4. Continue to rise while drawing the sword straight ahead, at an upward angle.

5. As soon as the sword tip clears the scabbard, step back with the left foot and strike forward with the sword tip to the height of an opponent's temple. The right hand should be about one fist width above the shoulder, extending almost straight ahead.

6. Move the left knee forward and down until it rests near the right foot. Begin to raise the sword overhead.

7. Move the left hand up to grasp the handle. Slide the right foot forward.

8. Cut straight down the center while pulling in with the right foot.

9. Perform chiburi by whipping the sword to the right at hip level. The sword should stop in a position pointing straight ahead and level with the ground. The tsuba should be even with the right knee, about fifteen centimeters to its right. Move the left hand back to press against the scabbard.

10. Grasp the scabbard with the left hand, forming a cradle at the opening with the thumb and forefinger. Move the sword across the front of the body until it rests on the finger cradle at a point on the blade about six inches from the tsuba. The sword should be level, its edge at about a 60° angle below straight up and down.

11. Slide the sword away from the body at a 45° angle until the tip reaches the opening of the scabbard. Keep it level.

12. Begin to slide the sword into the scabbard. At the same time, slide the right foot back until it is even with the left foot, then slide it out

to the right about ten inches. The right knee should move back and out.

13. When the right foot is set, move the left foot inward by pivoting on the knee. The inside edges of the feet should be touching. Let the left hand slide back when it is contacted by the scabbard. As soon as the sword is fully seated, place the thumb of the left hand on the tsuba.

14. Slide the right foot forward on a diagonal path until the right leg forms a right angle. Weight is still on the left knee.

15. Stand up by stepping forward with the left foot.

16. Move the right hand to the butt of the handle and grasp it there. Adjust the sword so that the handle meets the centerline of the body. Step back to the starting position moving the left foot first. At the starting position, move the right hand down to a relaxed position at the side of the body.

浮雲

Four • Floating Clouds

Yonhon Me • Ukigumo

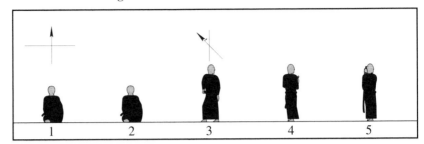

Scenario. An opponent grabs the sword handle of a seated swordsman. The swordsman stands and unbalances the opponent by pulling the handle across his own body. He then suddenly moves the handle forward, causing the attacker's grip to weaken, and draws the sword, cutting him in the process. Dropping to one knee, he pushes the sword horizontally across to cut the opponent, then steps back and finishes him with a downward cut. Flipping the blade to remove any blood, he resheathes his sword and stands up in a dignified manner.

1. Sit facing 90° to the left relative to the shomen.

2. Grasp the scabbard with the left hand.

3. Stand by rising onto the balls of the feet and stepping out toward the left rear. Pull the scabbard and sword back with the left hand. The right hand drops to a relaxed position at the side of the body.

4. Step across to the right front corner with the left foot while moving the scabbard and sword across the front of the body with the left hand. Move the right hand up to grasp the handle.

5. Begin drawing the sword upward with the right hand while pulling the scabbard down and back with the left.

6. As soon as the tip clears the opening of the scabbard, cut out to the right side by flipping the tip of the sword across the front of the body. Turn the left foot over in place so that the sole of the foot is facing upwards. Bend the knees and place the right knee against a point on the back of the left leg between knee and ankle.

7. Turn the body to face the right front corner while sinking onto the right knee. Reach out with the left hand to the back of the sword, about midway up the blade. Place the left hand against the back of the blade with the hand open, touching the blade with the flat of the hand between the thumb and forefinger.

8. Turn the blade over, using the left hand as a fulcrum. The edge should move to face toward the right, with the blade flat and the handle higher than the tip.

9. Cut horizontally across the front (from left front corner to right rear corner) by pushing with both hands.

10. Flip the tip toward the left rear, using the right hand as the center of rotation, by pushing the blade with the left hand. Once the sword faces backwards and upwards, grasp the handle with the left hand.

11. Turn to face directly toward the right front by moving the right leg back. Raise the sword to the overhead position. Slide the left foot forward.

12. Cut slightly off center so that the sword comes to rest outside (to the left of) the left leg.

13. Perform chiburi by whipping the sword to the right at hip level. The sword should stop in a position pointing straight ahead and level with the ground. The tsuba should about fifteen centimeters to the right of a line extending straight out from the right side of the hip. Move the left hand back to press against the scabbard.

14. Grasp the scabbard with the left hand, forming a cradle at the opening with the thumb and forefinger. Move the sword across the front of the body until it rests on the finger cradle at a point on the blade about six inches from the tsuba. The sword should be level, its edge at about a 60° angle below straight up and down.

15. Slide the sword away from the body at a 45° angle until the tip reaches the opening of the scabbard. Keep it level.

16. Begin to slide the sword into the scabbard. At the same time, slide the left foot back until it is even with the right foot, then slide it out to the left about ten inches. The left knee should move back and out.

17. When the left foot is set, move the right foot inward by pivoting on the knee. The inside edges of the feet should be touching. Let the left hand slide back when it is contacted by the scabbard. As soon as the sword is fully seated, place the thumb of the left hand on the tsuba.

18. Slide the left foot forward on a diagonal path until the left leg forms a right angle. Weight is still on the right knee.

19. Stand up by stepping forward with the right foot.

20. Move the right hand to the butt of the handle and grasp it there. Adjust the sword so that the handle meets the centerline of the body. Step back by stepping first with the right foot, to adjust the body to face straight ahead, then moving the left foot. At the starting position, move the right hand down to a relaxed position at the side of the body.

Five • Mountain Wind
Gohon Me • Oroshi

風

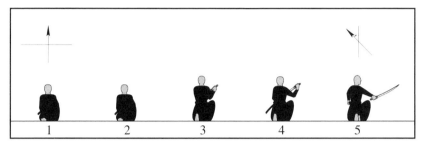

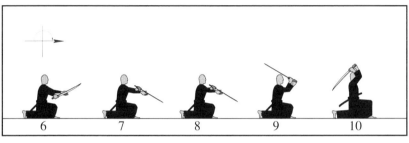

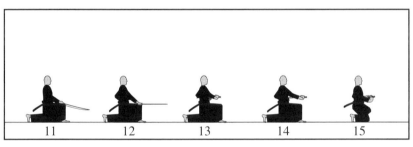

Scenario. While a swordsman sits, an opponent approaches and grabs the handle of his sword. The swordsman suddenly moves the handle forward, causing the attacker's grip to weaken, and draws the sword, cutting him in the process. Dropping to one knee, the swordsman pushes the sword horizontally across to cut the opponent, then steps back and finishes him with a downward cut. Flipping the blade to remove any blood, he resheathes his sword and stands up in a dignified manner.

139

1. Sit facing the left.

2. Grasp the scabbard with the left hand, then grasp the handle of the sword with the right.

3. Move the sword and scabbard down, then upwards in a circular motion from left to right. Step out with the right foot.

4. Begin to draw the sword up and to the right.

5. Cut to the right by flipping the tip across the front of the body with the right hand. Drive forward with the hips at the same time, turning the shoulders slightly to face the left rear corner.

6. Turn to face the shomen by moving the left foot back and reaching for the sword with the left hand. Place the left hand flat against the side of the blade.

7. Turn the blade over, using the left hand as a fulcrum. The edge should move to face toward the right, with the blade flat and the handle higher than the tip.

8. Cut horizontally across the front by pushing with both hands, moving the body toward the left by pushing with the left leg.

9. Flip the tip toward the rear, using the right hand as the center of rotation, by pushing the blade with the left hand. Once the sword faces back and up, grasp the handle with the left hand.

10. Turn to face directly toward the front by moving the left leg back. Raise the sword to the overhead position. Slide the right foot slightly forward.

11. Cut straight down the center.

12. Perform chiburi by whipping the sword to the right at hip level. The sword should stop in a position pointing straight ahead and level with the ground. The tsuba should be even with the right knee, about fifteen centimeters to its right. Move the left hand back to press against the scabbard.

13. Grasp the scabbard with the left hand, forming a cradle at the opening with the thumb and forefinger. Move the sword across the front of the body until it rests on the finger cradle at a point on the blade about six inches from the tsuba. The sword should be level, its edge at about a 60° angle below straight up and down.

14. Slide the sword away from the body at a 45° angle until the tip reaches the opening of the scabbard. Keep it level.

15. Begin to slide the sword into the scabbard. At the same time, slide the right foot back until it is even with the left foot, then slide it out to the right about ten inches. The right knee should move back and out.

16. When the right foot is set, move the left foot inward by pivoting on the knee. The inside edges of the feet should be touching. Let the left hand slide back when it is contacted by the scabbard. As soon as the sword is fully seated, place the thumb of the left hand on the tsuba.

18. Slide the right foot forward on a diagonal path until the right leg forms a right angle. Weight is still on the left knee.

19. Stand up by stepping forward with the left foot.

20. Move the right hand to the butt of the handle and grasp it there. Adjust the sword so that the handle meets the centerline of the body. Step back by moving the left foot first. At the starting position, move the right hand down to a relaxed position at the side of the body.

岩
波

Six • Breaking Waves

Roppon Me • Iwanami

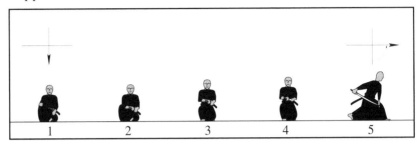

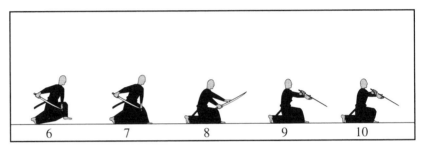

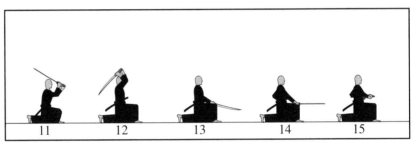

Scenario. While a swordsman sits, an opponent approaches from the side and grabs his scabbard. The swordsman grasps the attacker's hand and draws his sword, turning to face the opponent. Using the weight of his body to drive the sword, the swordsman thrusts the tip into his opponent's belly, cuts him with a horizontal stroke, then steps back and finishes him with a downward cut. Flipping the blade to remove any blood, he resheathes his sword and stands up in a dignified manner.

1. Sit facing the right.

2. Grasp the scabbard with the left hand, then grasp the handle of the sword with the right.

3. Begin to rise while drawing the sword straight ahead, parallel to the ground.

4. Continue drawing straight ahead. Slide the left foot backwards about twenty centimeters.

5. When the tip clears the opening of the scabbard, grasp it between the thumb and forefinger of the left hand. Turn to face the shomen by moving the left foot toward the back and pivoting on the right leg. Move both arms back to bring the tip even with the right knee.

6,7,8. Stomp by lifting the right leg off the ground without raising the hips or the body. When the foot hits the ground, drive forward with the sword and sink onto the left knee. The sword slides through the left hand so that it extends directly forward.

9. Turn the blade over, using the left hand as a fulcrum. The edge should move to face toward the right, with the blade flat and the handle higher than the tip.

10. Cut horizontally across the front by pushing with both hands, moving the body toward the left by pushing with the left leg.

11. Flip the tip toward the rear, using the right hand as the center of rotation, by pushing the blade with the left hand. Once the sword faces back and up, grasp the handle with the left hand.

12. Turn to face directly toward the front by moving the left leg back. Raise the sword to the overhead position. Slide the right foot slightly forward.

13. Cut straight down the center.

14. Perform chiburi by whipping the sword to the right at hip level. The sword should stop in a position pointing straight ahead and level with the ground. The tsuba should be even with the right knee, about fifteen centimeters to its right. Move the left hand back to press against the scabbard.

15. Grasp the scabbard with the left hand, forming a cradle at the opening with the thumb and forefinger. Move the sword across the front of the body until it rests on the finger cradle at a point on the blade about six inches from the tsuba. The sword should be level, its edge at about a 60° angle below straight up and down.

16. Slide the sword away from the body at a 45° angle until the tip reaches the opening of the scabbard. Keep it level.

17. Begin to slide the sword into the scabbard. At the same time, slide the right foot back until it is even with the left foot, then slide it out to the right about ten inches. The right knee moves back and out.

18. When the right foot is set, move the left foot inward by pivoting on the knee. The inside edges of the feet should be touching. Let the left hand slide back when it is contacted by the scabbard. As soon as the sword is fully seated, place the thumb of the left hand on the tsuba.

19. Slide the right foot forward on a diagonal path until the right leg forms a right angle. Weight is still on the left knee.

20. Stand up by stepping forward with the left foot.

21. Move the right hand to the butt of the handle and grasp it there. Adjust the sword so that the handle meets the centerline of the body. Step back by moving the left foot first. At the starting position, move the right hand down to a relaxed position at the side of the body.

Seven • Fish Scaling
Nanahon Me • Urokogaeshi

鱗
返

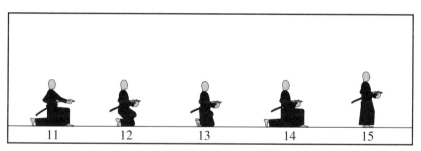

Scenario. A swordsman sits in the tatehiza position. When an opponent approaches from the side and prepares to attack, the swordsman turns and draws simultaneously, cutting the attacker in the process. He then drops onto one knee and finishes the opponent with a downward cut. Finally, he flips the blood off the sword, resheathes it, and stands up with dignity.

1. Sit facing to the right.

145

2. Grasp the scabbard with the left hand, then grasp the handle of the sword with the right.

3. Begin to rise while drawing the sword straight ahead, parallel to the ground.

4. Continue drawing while pivoting to face the front. Keep the knees bent.

5. Simultaneously step back with the left leg while drawing straight across the front. The right arm should end up 45° forward and level; sword should be level and point straight ahead. Pull the scabbard back with the left hand.

6. Slide the left knee forward until it is even with the right heel. At the same time, begin to raise the sword to the overhead position.

7. Move the left hand up to grasp the handle. Slide the right foot forward slightly.

8. Cut straight down the center.

9. Perform chiburi by whipping the sword to the right at hip level. The sword should stop in a position pointing straight ahead and level with the ground. The tsuba should be even with the right knee, about fifteen centimeters to its right. Move the left hand back to press against the scabbard.

10. Grasp the scabbard with the left hand, forming a cradle at the opening with the thumb and forefinger. Move the sword across the front of the body until it rests on the finger cradle at a point on the blade about six inches from the tsuba. The sword should be level, its edge at about a 60° angle below straight up and down.

11. Slide the sword away from the body at a 45° angle until the tip reaches the opening of the scabbard. Keep it level.

12. Begin to slide the sword into the scabbard. At the same time, slide the right foot back until it is even with the left foot, then slide it out to the right about ten inches. The right knee should move back and out.

13. When the right foot is set, move the left foot inward by pivoting on the knee. The inside edges of the feet should be touching. Let the left hand slide back when it is contacted by the scabbard. As soon as the sword is fully seated, place the thumb of the left hand on the tsuba.

14. Slide the right foot forward on a diagonal path until the right leg forms a right angle. Weight is still on the left knee.

15. Stand up by stepping forward with the left foot.

16. Move the right hand to the butt of the handle and grasp it there. Adjust the sword so that the handle meets the centerline of the body. Step back by moving the left foot first. At the starting position, move the right hand down to a relaxed position at the side of the body.

波
返

Eight • Returning Waves

Hachihon Me • Namigaeshi

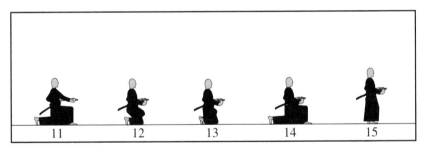

Scenario. A swordsman sits in the tatehiza position. When an opponent approaches from the rear and prepares to attack, the swordsman turns and draws simultaneously, cutting the attacker in the process. He then drops onto one knee and finishes the opponent with a downward cut. Finally, he flips the blood off the sword, resheathes it, and stands up with dignity.

1. Sit facing to the rear.

2. Grasp the scabbard with the left hand, then grasp the handle of the sword with the right.

3. Begin to rise onto the balls of the feet.

4. Continue drawing while pivoting to face the front. Begin drawing the sword straight ahead, about 30° above level. Keep the knees bent.

5. Simultaneously step back with the left leg while drawing straight across the front. The right arm should end up 45° forward and level; sword should be level and point straight ahead. Pull the scabbard back with the left hand.

6. Slide the left knee forward until it is even with the right heel. At the same time, begin to raise the sword to the overhead position.

7. Move the left hand up to grasp the handle near the butt. Slide the right foot forward slightly.

8. Cut straight down the center.

9. Perform chiburi by whipping the sword to the right at hip level. The sword should stop in a position pointing straight ahead and level with the ground. The tsuba should be even with the right knee, about fifteen centimeters to its right. Move the left hand back to press against the scabbard.

10. Grasp the scabbard with the left hand, forming a cradle at the opening with the thumb and forefinger. Move the sword across the front of the body until it rests on the finger cradle at a point on the blade about six inches from the tsuba. The sword should be level, its edge at about a 60° angle below straight up and down.

11. Slide the sword away from the body at a 45° angle until the tip reaches the opening of the scabbard. Keep it level.

12. Begin to slide the sword into the scabbard. At the same time, slide the right foot back until it is even with the left foot, then slide it out to the right about ten inches. The right knee should move back and out.

13. When the right foot is set, move the left foot inward by pivoting on the knee. The inside edges of the feet should be touching. Let the left hand slide back when it is contacted by the scabbard. As soon as the sword is fully seated, place the thumb of the left hand on the tsuba.

14. Slide the right foot forward on a diagonal path until the right leg forms a right angle. Weight is still on the left knee.

15. Stand up by stepping forward with the left foot.

16. Move the right hand to the butt of the handle. Grasp the handle at that point. Adjust the sword so that the handle meets the centerline of the body. Step back by moving the left foot first. At the starting position, move the right hand down to a relaxed position at the side of the body.

Nine • Waterfall

Kyuhon Me • Takiotoshi

瀧
落

Scenario. A swordsman sits in the tatehiza position. An opponent approaches from the rear and grasps the end of his scabbard. The swordsman stands, throwing the attacker off balance by turning and lifting the scabbard, then forces the attacker to release his grip by stepping forward and moving the scabbard in a large circle. He then turns, draws, thrusts the sword into his opponent's belly, and drops onto one knee to finish the opponent with a downward cut. Finally, he flips the blood off the sword, resheathes it, and stands up with dignity.

151

1. Sit facing to the rear.

2. Grasp the scabbard with the left hand.

3. Step onto the ball of the left foot and begin to rise, simultaneously rotating the sword in toward the body and pressing down on the scabbard with the left hand.

4. Stand up fully and look back over the left shoulder. Continue to rotate and press down on the handle of the sword. Let the right hand relax at the side of the body.

5. Step forward with the left foot while bringing the sword and scabbard up to the center in a circular motion.

6. Step forward with the right foot. Bring the sword and scabbard down and forward until they are nearly level.

7. Begin to draw the sword straight ahead, level with the floor. Pull the scabbard back with the left hand.

8. As soon as the tip of the sword clears the scabbard, pivot to face the front by turning to the left. Pivot on the right heel, then the left heel. Pull the scabbard fully back with the left hand and keep the sword close the the body with the right. Sword should be level and the right hand should be behind the hip.

9. Adjust the body to face fully forward by stepping slightly to the left with the left foot and back and slightly to the right with the right foot. Thrust forward with the tip of the sword.

10. Bring the sword back to chudan position and grasp the handle near the butt with the left hand.

11. Raise the sword to the overhead position while stepping forward with the right foot, which should move to about half a foot's length further back than the left.

12. Step out with the right foot and cut straight down while sinking onto the left knee.

13. Perform chiburi by whipping the sword to the right at hip level. The sword should stop in a position pointing straight ahead and level with the ground. The tsuba should be even with the right knee, about fifteen centimeters to its right. Move the left hand back to press against the scabbard.

14. Grasp the scabbard with the left hand, forming a cradle at the opening with the thumb and forefinger. Move the sword across the front of the body until it rests on the finger cradle at a point on the blade about six inches from the tsuba. The sword should be level, its edge at about a 60° angle below straight up and down.

15. Slide the sword away from the body at a 45° angle until the tip reaches the opening of the scabbard. Keep it level.

16. Begin to slide the sword into the scabbard. At the same time, slide the right foot back until it is even with the left foot, then slide it out to the right about ten inches. The right knee should move back and out.

17. When the right foot is set, move the left foot inward by pivoting on the knee. The inside edges of the feet should be touching. Let the left hand slide back when it is contacted by the scabbard. As soon as the sword is fully seated, place the thumb of the left hand on the tsuba.

18. Slide the right foot forward on a diagonal path until the right leg forms a right angle. Weight is still on the left knee.

19. Stand up by stepping forward with the left foot.

20. Move the right hand to the butt of the handle and grasp it there. Adjust the sword so that the handle meets the centerline of the body. Step back by moving the left foot first. At the starting position, move the right hand down to a relaxed position at the side of the body.

Ten • Facing Front

Jippon Me • Makkoh

真
向

Scenario. The swordsman sits, facing his opponent. Just as the opponent is about to attack, the swordsman draws and finishes him with a downward cut. He then flips the blood off his sword by whipping it to the side, and resheathes it with dignity.

1. Sit in seiza, facing straight ahead.

2. Grasp the scabbard with the left hand and the handle of the sword in the right.

3. Begin to draw in an upward direction, straight ahead, while rising onto the knees. Move onto the balls of the feet.

4. Draw the sword upwards to protect the head. Pull back on the scabbard with the left hand.

5. Raise the sword to the overhead position. Move the left hand up to grasp the handle.

6. Cut straight down the center. While cutting, rise slightly off the knees and let the weight of the body fall to drive the cut.

7. Perform chiburi by whipping the sword to the right at hip level. The sword should stop in a position pointing straight ahead and level with the ground. The tsuba should be even with the right knee, about fifteen centimeters to its right. Move the left hand back to press against the scabbard.

8. Grasp the scabbard with the left hand, forming a cradle at the opening with the thumb and forefinger. Move the sword across the front of the body until it rests on the finger cradle at a point on the blade about six inches from the tsuba. The sword should be level, its edge at about a 60° angle below straight up and down.

9. Slide the sword away from the body at a 45° angle until the tip reaches the opening of the scabbard. Keep it level.

10. Begin to slide the sword into the scabbard. At the same time, slide the right foot back until it is even with the left foot, then slide it to the right about ten inches. The right knee moves back and out.

11. When the right foot is set, move the left foot inward by pivoting on the knee. The inside edges of the feet should be touching. Let the left hand slide back when it is contacted by the scabbard. As soon as the sword is fully seated, place the thumb of the left hand on the tsuba.

12. Slide the right foot forward on a diagonal path until the right leg forms a right angle. Weight is still on the left knee.

13. Stand up by stepping forward with the left foot.

14. Move the right hand to the butt of the handle. Grasp the handle at that point. Adjust the sword so that the handle meets the centerline of the body. Step back by moving the left foot first. At the starting position, move the right hand down to a relaxed position at the side of the body.

Secret Forms, Standing Set

The techniques of the Standing Set (*Tachiwaza no Bu*) are quite advanced, in that they all deal with specific scenarios that require special methods of drawing, cutting, or stepping. A student well versed in the basics of sword handling will not find the forms especially difficult to learn, but any weaknesses will become apparent quickly in the more esoteric motions. It is important for the student to study each special method and practice it repeatedly until it can be performed with ease.

In Eishin-Ryu, the set name Tachiwaza no Bu is a slight misnomer, since the last three forms included in this set, called *Itomagoi*, are done from the seiza position. They are variations on the same theme, which is a bow interrupted by an attack from the person to whom one is bowing. The three Itomagoi forms are excellent tools for teaching quick response and control of the body's weight from a kneeling position. The names of the Tachiwaza no Bu forms are as follows:

1.	Accompaniment	*Yukizure*	157
2.	Companions	*Tsuredachi*	159
3.	Complete Resolution	*So Makuri*	161
4.	Full Stop	*So Dome*	164
5.	Loyal Retainer	*Shinobu*	167
6.	Misdirection	*Yukichigai*	169
7.	Sleeve Flip	*Sodesuri Gaeshi*	171
8.	Entering the Gate	*Moniri*	173
9.	Between Walls	*Kabezoi*	175
10.	Parrying	*Ukenagashi*	177
11.	Farewell Visit One	*Itomagoi Sono Ichi*	179
12.	Farewell Visit Two	*Itomagoi Sono Ni*	181
13.	Farewell Visit Three	*Itomagoi Sono San*	184

One • Accompaniment

Ippon Me • Yukizure

行
連

Scenario. A swordsman walks between two opponents, one on each side. As they move forward, the swordsman takes a smaller step to allow the others to get ahead, then steps out and draws to cut the opponent on his right before turning to finish the opponent on the left with a downward cut. Finally, he flips the blood off his blade and resheathes it with dignity.

1. Stand facing the shomen. Shoulders should be pulled back and down, hands held relaxed at the sides.

2. Step forward with the right foot. Let the left arm swing forward.

3. Step forward with the left foot, letting the right arm swing forward.

4. Step forward with the right foot while grasping the scabbard with the left hand.

157

5. Take a half step forward with the left foot. Grasp the handle of the sword with the right hand.

6. Begin to draw the sword, upward and toward the right front corner.

7. Take a large step toward the right front corner while cutting on a diagonal path in the same direction. Extend out with the sword tip while pulling the scabbard back with the left hand.

8. Move to face the left front corner by stepping across the front with the right foot. Raise the sword to the overhead position and move the left hand up to grasp the handle.

9. Cut straight down toward the left front corner.

10. Perform chiburi by whipping the sword to the side at hip level. The right hand should be forward of the body, the sword level and pointing straight ahead. Move the left hand back to press against the scabbard.

11. Grasp the scabbard with the left hand, forming a cradle at the opening with the thumb and forefinger. Move the sword across the front of the body until it rests on the finger cradle at a point on the blade about six inches from the tsuba. The sword should be level, its edge at about a $60°$ angle below straight up and down.

12. Slide the sword away from the body at a $45°$ angle until the tip reaches the opening of the scabbard. Keep it level.

13. Begin to slide the sword into the scabbard. Once the tip is inside the scabbard, move the first two-thirds of the blade into the scabbard in one quick motion. Finish moving the sword inward very slowly. Let the left hand slide back when it is contacted by the scabbard. As soon as the sword is fully seated, place the thumb of the left hand on the tsuba.

14. Step forward with the left foot.

15. Move the right hand to the butt of the handle and grasp it there. Adjust the sword so that the handle meets the centerline of the body. Step back to the starting position moving, the left foot first to adjust the body to face forward. At the starting position, move the right hand down to a relaxed position at the side of the body.

Two • Companions
Nihon Me • Tsuredachi

連達

Scenario. A swordsman walks between two opponents, one just ahead and right, the other just behind and left. As they walk, the swordsman draws and thrusts into the opponent on the left before turning to finish the opponent on the right with a downward cut. Finally, he flips the blood off his blade and resheathes it with dignity.

1. Stand facing the shomen. Shoulders should be pulled back and down, hands held relaxed at the sides.

2. Step forward with the right foot. Let the left arm swing forward.

3. Step forward with the left foot, letting the right arm swing forward.

4. Step forward with the right foot while grasping the scabbard with the left hand.

5. Step forward with the left foot. Grasp the handle of the sword with the right hand.

6. Take a large step toward the right front corner with the right foot. Rotate the sword and scabbard until the blade is flat. Begin to draw, level with the floor, toward the right front corner.

7. Continue to draw until only the tip remains inside the scabbard.

8. Look back over the left shoulder. To clear the tip, pull the scabbard fully back with the left hand until it is perpendicular with the path of the sword. Thrust toward the left rear corner with the sword. Stop when the tsuba is even with the left pectoral muscle.

9. Look toward the right front while raising the sword to the overhead position.

10. Cut straight down toward the right front corner.

11–16. Perform chiburi and finish as in Yukizure (p. 157), adjusting the body to face straight ahead by stepping back with the right foot first.

Three • Complete Resolution

Sanbon Me • So Makuri

| 1 | 2 | 3 | 4 | 5 |

| 6 | 7 | 8 | 9 | 10 |

| 11 | 12 | 13 | 14 | 15 |

| 16 | 17 | 18 | 19 | 20 |

| 21 | 22 | 23 | 24 | 25 |

惣
捲

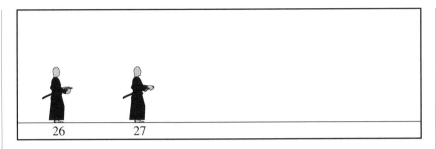

26   27

Scenario. A swordsman faces an opponent. As they approach each other, and the opponent attacks, the swordsman draws, parrying the cut, and strikes the opponent's temple. He follows up with two angular cuts to the opponent's body, one horizontal cut, and finishes him with a downward cut. Finally, he flips the blood off his blade and resheathes it with dignity.

1. Stand facing the shomen. Shoulders should be pulled back and down, hands held relaxed at the sides.

2. Step forward with the right foot. Let the left arm swing forward.

3. Step forward with the left foot, letting the right arm swing forward.

4. Step forward with the right foot while grasping the scabbard with the left hand.

5. Step forward with the left foot. Grasp the handle of the sword with the right hand.

6. Step forward with the right foot while drawing the sword about one foot straight ahead.

7. Step back with the right foot while drawing the sword upward, directly into the overhead position. Steps 7, 8 and 9 should be performed as one integrated motion.

8. Step forward with the right foot.

9. Bring the left foot forward until it is about one-half foot's length further back than the right while striking straight ahead to forehead height. Extend forward with the tip.

10. Raise the sword to the overhead position.

11. Step forward with the right foot.

12. Bring the left foot forward as in step 9 while cutting on the kesa angle, left to right. Step when the sword is parallel to the floor.

13. Raise the sword to the overhead position.

14. Step forward with the right foot.

15. Bring the left foot forward as in the previous two moves while cutting on a low kesa (abdomen height), from right to left. Stop the sword when it is parallel to the floor.

16. Lift the sword tip straight up. Bring the tsuba up until it is even with the chin.

17. Lower the sword to the left side of the body, edge facing outward, until it is parallel to the floor.

18–21. Take a large step forward with the right foot while slowly cutting in a horizontal path across the front of the body. Continue the cut in a circular motion to raise the sword to the overhead position and then cut straight down center.

22–27. Perform chiburi and finish as in Yukizure (p. 157).

惣
留

Four · Full Stop
Yonhon Me · So Dome

Scenario. A swordsman faces an opponent. They approach each other and, when the opponent attacks, the swordsman flips his sword out and stops the attack by placing it on the opponent's wrists. Twice more, the opponent tries to attack, and each time the swordsman stops him in the same manner, causing him to give up. Finally, the swordsman flips the blood off his blade and resheathes it with dignity.

1. Stand facing the shomen. Shoulders should be pulled back and down, hands held relaxed at the sides.

2. Step forward with the right foot. Let the left arm swing forward.

3. Step forward with the left foot, letting the right arm swing forward.

4. Step forward with the right foot while grasping the scabbard with the left hand.

5. Take a half step forward with the left foot. Grasp the handle of the sword with the right hand.

6. Begin to draw the sword toward a point directly in front of the left shoulder.

7. Step out with the right foot, cutting on a diagonal path toward the front. Extend the tip to about the height of an opponent's wrist. The right arm should extend down toward the right and the sword should extend up toward the left at an angle of about 45°. The left hand moves back to press against the scabbard at the point where it intersects the obi.

8. Bring the left foot even with the right. Grasp the scabbard with the left hand, forming a cradle at the opening with the thumb and forefinger. Move the sword across the front of the body until it rests on the finger cradle at a point on the blade about six inches from the tsuba.

9. Slide the sword away from the body at a 45° angle until the tip reaches the opening of the scabbard. Keep it level.

10. Begin to slide the sword into the scabbard. Once the tip is inside the scabbard, move the first two-thirds of the blade into the scabbard in one quick motion. Finish moving the sword inward very slowly.

11, 12. Repeat the drawing motion as in steps 6 and 7.

13–15. Repeat the sheathing motion as in steps 8 through 10.

16, 17. Repeat the drawing motion as in steps 6 and 7.

18–23. Perform chiburi and finish as in Yukizure (p. 157).

Five • Loyal Retainer

Gohon Me • Shinobu

信
夫

Scenario. A swordsman stalks a sentry at night, in an area with many obstructions. Spying the sentry, he silently draws his sword and raises it overhead, then lets it move toward the ground in a large circle. He taps the ground with the tip of his sword, and when the sentry turns toward the sound, the swordsman cuts him in two with a downward stroke. Finally, he flips the blood off his blade and resheathes it with dignity.

1. Stand facing the shomen. Shoulders should be pulled back and down, hands held relaxed at the sides.

2. Step forward with the right foot. Let the left arm swing forward.

3. Step forward with the left foot, letting the right arm swing forward.

4. Step forward with the right foot while grasping the scabbard with the left hand.

5. Step toward the left front corner with the left foot. Grasp the handle of the sword with the right hand.

6. Slide the right foot straight ahead while drawing the sword toward the front at an upward angle. Lean the body toward the right.

7. When the sword clears the scabbard, raise it overhead along the left side of the body.

8. Move the sword in a slow arc around the back and down along the right side of the body until the tip is pointing downward and slightly ahead.

9. Straighten the body and swing the sword to the overhead position along the right side while stepping toward the right front corner with the left foot. Move the left hand up to grasp the handle.

10. Step forward with the right foot (toward the right front) and cut straight down.

11–16. Perform chiburi and finish as in Yukizure (p. 157). Step back with the right foot first to adjust the body to face forward.

Six • Misdirection

Roppon Me • Yukichigai

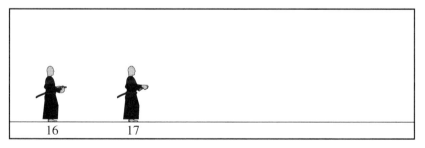

Scenario. A swordsman walks between two opponents, one in front, one behind. At a moment of opportunity, the swordsman strikes the forward opponent with the butt of the handle to disturb his balance, then turns and cuts the rear opponent with a downward stroke before turning back to the front to finish off the opponent there. Finally, he flips the blood off his blade and resheathes it with dignity.

1. Stand facing the shomen. Shoulders should be pulled back and down, hands held relaxed at the sides.

2. Step forward with the right foot. Let the left arm swing forward.

3. Step forward with the left foot, letting the right arm swing forward.

4. Step forward with the right foot while grasping the scabbard with the left hand.

5. Step forward with the left foot. Grasp the handle of the sword with the right hand and move it downward with a short, sharp motion.

6. Step forward with the right foot while moving the sword and scabbard toward the front at an upward angle.

7. Turn 180° to the left while lowering the hips and moving the scabbard down to draw the sword.

8. When the sword clears the scabbard, raise it to the overhead position. Move the left hand up to grasp the handle.

9. Shift slightly forward on the left leg and cut straight down.

10. Turn 180° to the right while raising the sword overhead.

11. Shift slightly forward on the right leg and cut straight down.

12–17. Perform chiburi and finish as in Yukizure (p. 157). Move the right hand down to the side of the body after reaching the starting position.

Seven • Sleeve Flip

Nanahon Me • Sodesuri Gaeshi

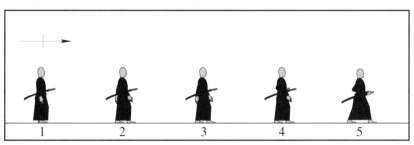

袖摺返

Scenario. A swordsman walks in a group of allies. He sees an opponent preparing to attack, and moves toward the edge of his group before drawing his sword. Then, just at the opponent seems ready to draw his own sword, the swordsman uses the flat of his blade to push his allies back out of harm's way before stepping forward to cut the opponent down. Finally, he flips the blood off his blade and resheathes it with dignity.

171

1. Stand facing the shomen. Shoulders should be pulled back and down, hands held relaxed at the sides.

2. Step forward with the right foot. Let the left arm swing forward.

3. Step forward with the left foot, letting the right arm swing forward.

4. Step forward with the right foot while grasping the scabbard with the left hand.

5. Step forward with the left foot. Grasp the handle of the sword with the right hand.

6. Step forward with the right foot while beginning to draw the sword on a level path, straight ahead. Pull the scabbard back with the left hand.

7. Continue drawing straight ahead until the sword clears the scabbard.

8. Bring the right foot back, even with the left, and raise the sword hand so that the hands are crossed at the wrists. The sword should rest on the sleeve of the left arm, at a point midway between the shoulder and elbow. Slide the right thumb back to press against the side of the handle, to keep the sword blade flat (straight up and down) for the next two motions.

9. Rise onto the toes and raise the wrists up to the level of the top of the head.

10. Simultaneously drop and slide the right foot forward while expanding outward with both hands. The sword should move on a horizontal path until it points directly out to the right.

11. Step forward with the left foot and continue the motion of both hands until the sword reaches the overhead position. Grasp the handle with the left hand.

12. Step forward with the right foot, then cut straight down the center.

13–18. Perform chiburi and finish as in Yukizure (p.157).

Eight • Entering the Gate

Hachihon Me • Moniri

Scenario. A swordsman stands on one side of an entrance (a door or gate). Two opponents face him, one in front, on the other side of the gate, and another behind the swordsman. The swordsman approaches the gate, drawing his sword just as he passes through, then thrusts it into the opponent on the other side. Then, turning to go back through the gate, he raises the sword so that it brushes the top of the gate. The moment it clears the top, he strikes down the opponent who was at his rear. He then turns back toward the injured

173

opponent in front, again holding the sword up, and finishes him with a strike at the moment the sword clears the top of the gate. Finally, he flips the blood off his blade and resheathes it with dignity.

1. Stand facing the shomen. Shoulders should be pulled back and down, hands held relaxed at the sides.

2. Step forward with the right foot. Let the left arm swing forward.

3. Step forward with the left foot, letting the right arm swing forward.

4. Step forward with the right foot while grasping the scabbard with the left hand.

5. Step forward with the left foot. Grasp the handle of the sword with the right hand.

6. Step forward with the right foot while beginning to draw the sword on a level path, straight ahead. Pull the scabbard back with the left hand.

7. Draw straight ahead until the sword clears the scabbard.

8. Step forward with the left foot and pull the scabbard fully back against the body with the left hand. Move the sword so that the tip is forward and the handle is back, just above hip level.

9. Take a large step forward with the right foot and thrust straight ahead with the sword at chest height.

10. Turn 180° to the left and raise the sword overhead, keeping the tip higher than the handle. Move the left hand up to grasp the handle.

11. Shift slightly forward on the left foot and cut straight down.

12. Turn 180° to the right and raise the sword overhead, keeping the tip higher than the handle.

13. Shift slightly forward on the right foot and cut down center.

14–19. Perform chiburi and finish as in Yukizure (p. 157).

Nine • Between Walls

Kyuhon Me • Kabezoi

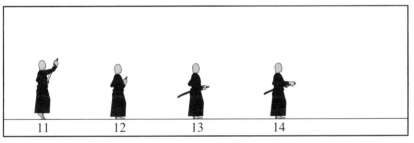

Scenario. A swordsman, walking in a narrow corridor between two buildings, encounters an opponent. As the opponent attacks, the swordsman draws his sword and blocks the attack, then cuts the opponent in two with a downward stroke. He then flips the blood off his blade and resheathes it with dignity.

1. Stand facing the shomen. Shoulders should be pulled back and down, hands held relaxed at the sides.

2. Step forward with the right foot. Let the left arm swing forward.

3. Step forward with the left foot, letting the right arm swing forward.

4. Step forward with the right foot while grasping the scabbard with the left hand.

5. Bring the left foot forward until it is even with the right foot. Grasp the handle of the sword with the right hand.

6. Rise onto the balls of the feet while drawing the sword upward. Pull down on the scabbard with the left hand.

7. Raise the sword to the overhead position. Move the left hand up to grasp the handle.

8. Cut straight down the center.

9. Perform chiburi by whipping the sword to the side while maintaining its downward angle. Move the left hand back to press against the scabbard.

10. Grasp the end of the scabbard with the left hand, forming a cradle at the opening with the thumb and forefinger. Bring the sword up to rest on the cradle.

11. Slide the blade along the cradle while raising the handle until the tip clears the opening of the scabbard.

12. Resheathe the sword in a downward direction, quickly as in the other forms of this set, and slowly drop into a regular standing position while resheathing the last three inches of the blade.

13. Move the handle down to bring the sheathed sword to the regular position alongside the body.

14. Move the right hand to the end of the handle. Adjust the sword and scabbard back to the centered position. Step back to the starting position, left foot first. At the starting position, move the right hand down to a relaxed position at the side of the body.

Ten • Parrying
Jippon Me • Ukenagashi

受
流

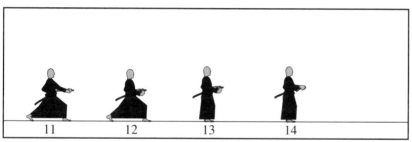

Scenario. A swordsman faces an opponent. They approach each other and, when the opponent attacks, the swordsman draws and parries the attack by raising his sword overhead. The momentum of the opponent's attack carries him past the swordsman to the left, and the swordsman turns to track him, finishing him with a downward stroke. Finally, the swordsman flips the blood off his blade and resheathes it with dignity.

1. Stand facing the shomen. Shoulders should be pulled back and down, hands held relaxed at the sides.

2. Step forward with the right foot. Let the left arm swing forward.

3. Step forward with the left foot, letting the right arm swing forward.

177

4. Step forward with the right foot while grasping the scabbard with the left hand.

5. Step forward and across to the right front corner with the left foot. Begin to draw the sword toward the right front corner, on a level path.

6. As soon as the sword clears the scabbard, lift it to protect the head. The koshi of the sword should be immediately in front of and above the head. The tip extends toward the left, slightly toward the rear. Pull the scabbard back with the left hand.

7. Move the left shoulder and hip back to bring the sword to the overhead position. Move the left hand up to grasp the handle.

8. Cut straight down toward the left front corner.

9–14. Perform chiburi and finish as in Yukizure (p. 157). Step back with the left foot first to adjust to body to face directly forward.

Eleven • Farewell Visit One

Juippon Me • Itomagoi Sono Ichi

暇
乞
其
の
一

Scenario. A swordsman sits, facing an official, who is also seated. The swordsman begins to bow but, as he does, he notices that the official is drawing his sword. The swordsman then draws his sword, parries the cut, and finishes the opponent with a downward cut. Finally, he flips the blood off his blade and resheathes it with dignity.

1. Sit in seiza, facing straight ahead.

2. Lower the head as if beginning to bow.

3. Grasp the scabbard with the left hand and the handle of the sword in the right.

4. Begin to draw in an upward direction, toward center, while rising onto the knees. Move onto the balls of the feet. Do not move the knees together.

179

5. Continue drawing the sword until it clears the scabbard. Pull back on the scabbard with the left hand.

6. Raise the sword to the overhead position. Move the left hand up to grasp the handle.

7. Cut straight down the center. While cutting, rise slightly off the knees and let the weight of the body fall to drive the cut.

8. Perform chiburi by whipping the sword to the side at hip level. The right hand should be forward of the body, the sword level and pointing straight ahead. Move the left hand back to press against the scabbard.

9. Grasp the scabbard with the left hand, forming a cradle at the opening with the thumb and forefinger. Move the sword across the front of the body until it rests on the finger cradle at a point on the blade about six inches from the tsuba. The sword should be level, its edge at about a 60° angle below straight up and down.

10. Slide the sword away from the body at a 45° angle until the tip reaches the opening of the scabbard. Keep it level.

11. Begin to slide the sword into the scabbard. Once the tip is inside the scabbard, move the first two-thirds of the blade into the scabbard in one quick motion. Finish moving the sword inward very slowly. Let the left hand slide back when it is contacted by the scabbard. As soon as the sword is fully seated, place the thumb of the left hand on the tsuba.

12. Slide the knees toward one another, so that they end up about two fist lengths apart.

13. Move the right hand to the butt of the handle.

14. Drop slowly into the seiza position.

15. Adjust the sword so that the handle meets the centerline of the body, then move the hands to rest on the thighs, as in the starting position.

Twelve • Farewell Visit Two

Junihon Me • Itomagoi Sono Ni

暇乞其の二

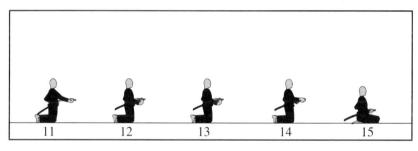

Scenario. A swordsman sits, facing an official who is also seated. The swordsman begins to bow but, as he does, he notices that the official is drawing his sword. The swordsman then draws his sword, parries the cut, and finishes the opponent with a downward cut. Finally, he flips the blood off his blade and resheathes it with dignity.

1. Sit in seiza, facing straight ahead.

2. Lower the head and move the left hand forward as if beginning to bow.

3. Continue the bowing motion by moving the right hand forward. Both hands should stop with the fingertips touching the floor.

4. Grasp the scabbard with the left hand and the handle of the sword with the right.

5. Straighten the body and begin to draw in an upward direction, toward center, while rising onto the knees. Move onto the balls of the feet. Do not move the knees together.

6. Continue drawing the sword until it clears the scabbard. Pull back on the scabbard with the left hand.

7. Raise the sword to the overhead position. Move the left hand up to grasp the handle.

8. Cut straight down the center. While cutting, rise slightly off the knees and let the weight of the body fall to drive the cut.

9. Perform chiburi by whipping the sword to the side at hip level. The right hand should be forward of the body, the sword level and pointing straight ahead. Move the left hand back to press against the scabbard.

10. Grasp the scabbard with the left hand, forming a cradle at the opening with the thumb and forefinger. Move the sword across the front of the body until it rests on the finger cradle at a point on the blade about six inches from the tsuba. The sword should be level, its edge at about a $60°$ angle below straight up and down.

11. Slide the sword away from the body at a $45°$ angle until the tip reaches the opening of the scabbard. Keep it level.

12. Begin to slide the sword into the scabbard. Once the tip is inside the scabbard, move the first two-thirds of the blade into the scabbard in one quick motion. Finish moving the sword inward very slowly. Let the left hand slide back when it is contacted

by the scabbard. As soon as the sword is fully seated, place the thumb of the left hand on the tsuba.

13. Slide the knees toward one another, so that they end up about two fist lengths apart.

14. Move the right hand to the butt of the handle.

15. Drop slowly into the seiza position.

16. Adjust the sword so that the handle meets the centerline of the body, then move the hands to rest on the thighs, as in the starting position.

暇
乞
其
の
三

Thirteen • Farewell Visit Three

Jusanbon Me • Itomagoi Sono San

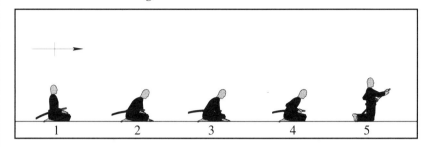

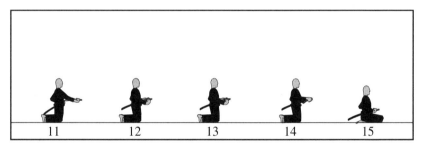

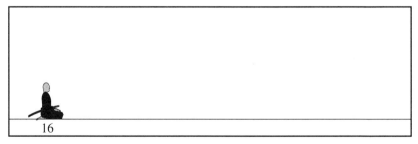

Scenario. A swordsman sits, facing an official who is also seated. The swordsman begins to bow but, as he does, he notices that the official is drawing his sword. The swordsman then draws his own sword, parries the cut, and finishes the opponent with a downward cut. Finally, he flips the blood off his blade and resheathes it with dignity.

1. Sit in seiza, facing straight ahead.

2. Lower the head and move the left hand foward as if beginning to bow.

3. Complete the bowing motion by moving the right hand forward. Both hands should come to a stop flat on the floor.

4. Grasp the scabbard with the left hand and the handle of the sword in the right.

5. Straighten the body and begin to draw in an upward direction, toward center, while rising onto the knees. Move onto the balls of the feet. Do not move the knees together.

6. Continue drawing the sword until it clears the scabbard. Pull back on the scabbard with the left hand.

7. Raise the sword to the overhead position. Move the left hand up to grasp the handle.

8. Cut straight down the center. While cutting, rise slightly off the knees and let the weight of the body fall to drive the cut.

9. Perform chiburi by whipping the sword to the side at hip level. The right hand should be forward of the body, the sword level and pointing straight ahead. Move the left hand back to press against the scabbard.

10. Grasp the scabbard with the left hand, forming a cradle at the opening with the thumb and forefinger. Move the sword across the front of the body until it rests on the finger cradle at a point on the blade about six inches from the tsuba. The sword should be level, its edge at about a 60° angle below straight up and down.

11. Slide the sword away from the body at a 45° angle until the tip reaches the opening of the scabbard. Keep it level.

12. Begin to slide the sword into the scabbard. Once the tip is inside the scabbard, move the first two-thirds of the blade into the scabbard in one quick motion. Finish moving the sword inward very slowly. Let the left hand slide back when it is contacted

by the scabbard. As soon as the sword is fully seated, place the thumb of the left hand on the tsuba.

13. Slide the knees toward one another, so that they end up about two fist lengths apart.

14. Move the right hand to the butt of the handle.

15. Drop slowly into the seiza position.

16. Adjust the sword so that the handle meets the centerline of the body, then move the hands to rest on the thighs, as in the starting position.

Advanced Techniques

Secret Forms,
Seated Set

The techniques in this advanced set (*Okuiai, Iwaza no Bu*) combine the character and efficiency of the tatehiza forms with the fast noto of other secret sets. Many of these techniques are designed to work in areas with obstructions: under a ledge, in a doorway, in a narrow hall or alley. For that reason, they employ some unique drawing methods and unique styles of moving into a cut.

The student should be competent at the basic tatehiza set before any attempt is made to learn this set, since any weaknesses that remain will be carried over into practice of these forms. Two years practice of the ten forms of Tatehiza no Bu are recommended before moving on to this set. The names of the forms are as follows:

1. Mist	*Kasumi*	190
2. Encircled Leg	*Sunegakoi*	193
3. Blocked at the Door	*Tozume*	195
4. Beneath the Doorway	*Towaki*	197
5. Four Directional Cut	*Shihogiri*	199
6. Beneath the Ledge	*Tanashita*	201
7. Blocked on Both Sides	*Ryozume*	203
8. Charging the Tiger	*Torabashiri*	205

奥居合居業の部

One • Mist
Ippon Me • Kasumi

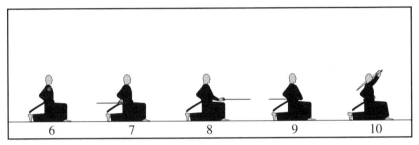

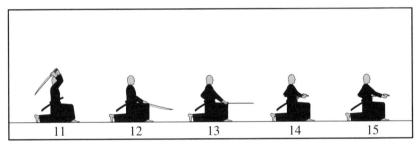

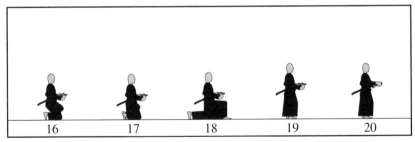

Scenario. A swordsman sits facing an opponent. As the opponent moves to attack, the swordsman draws and cuts him across the throat, then reverses the direction of the stroke to cut his forward knee. The swordsman then finishes his opponent with a downward cut, flips the blood off his sword and resheathes it before standing up with dignity.

1. Sit facing the shomen, left left tucked under the body and right foot tucked near the left knee. The right knee should be up, so that the

leg makes a 45° angle upward toward the right. The left fist rests near the hip joint of the left leg; the right fist rests atop the right knee.

2. Grasp the handle of the sword with the right hand, the scabbard with the left, and rotate them outward slightly while moving the left knee inward.

3. Begin to rise onto the left knee while beginning to draw the sword toward throat level.

4. Step out with the right foot and draw straight across the front of the body. Pull the scabbard back with the left hand.

5, 6. Continue the horizontal motion until the sword extends straight out to the right.

7. Rotate the right hand 180° clockwise and lower it until the sword is pointing straight back, parallel to the floor at hip level.

8, 9. Cut back across the front of the body at knee level, moving the sword in a horizontal arc until it points almost straight back on the left.

10, 11. Continue the motion by raising the sword to the overhead position. Move the left hand up to grasp the handle. Slide the right foot slightly forward.

12. Cut straight down center while pulling in with the right foot.

13. Perform chiburi by whipping the sword to the right at hip level. The sword should stop in a position pointing straight ahead and level with the ground. The tsuba should be even with the right knee, about fifteen centimeters to its right. Move the left hand back to press against the scabbard.

14. Grasp the scabbard with the left hand, forming a cradle at the opening with the thumb and forefinger. Move the sword across the front of the body until it rests on the cradle at a point on the blade about six inches from the tsuba. The sword should be level, its edge at about a 60° angle below straight up and down.

15. Slide the sword away from the body at a 45° angle until the tip reaches the opening of the scabbard. Keep it level.

16. Begin to slide the sword into the scabbard. Once the tip is inside the scabbard, move the first two-thirds of the blade into the scabbard in one quick motion. Finish moving the sword inward very slowly. At the same time, slide the right foot back until it is even with the left foot, then slide it out to the right about ten inches. The right knee should move back and out. Let the left hand slide back when it is contacted by the scabbard. As soon as the sword is fully seated, place the thumb of the left hand on the tsuba.

17. When the right foot is set, move the left foot inward by pivoting on the knee. The inside edges of the feet should be touching. Let the left hand slide back when it is contacted by the tsuba. As soon as the sword is fully seated, place the thumb of the left hand on the tsuba.

18. Slide the right foot forward on a diagonal path until the right leg forms a right angle. Weight is still on the left knee.

19. Stand up by stepping forward with the left leg.

20. Move the right hand to the butt of the handle and grasp it there. Adjust the sword so that the handle meets the centerline of the body. Step back to the starting position moving the left foot first. At the starting position, move the right hand down to a relaxed position at the side of the body.

Two • Encircled Leg

Nihon Me • Sunegakoi

Scenario. A swordsman sits facing an opponent. As the opponent moves to attack his leg, the swordsman rises to draw and parry the attack, but his rear leg gets caught by something. Instead of struggling to free his leg, however, the swordsman drops in place, finishes his opponent with a downward cut, flips the blood off the sword and resheathes it. His motions having freed his leg, he stands up with dignity.

1. Sit facing the shomen, left left tucked under the body and right foot tucked near the left knee. The right knee should be up, so that the leg makes a 45° angle upward toward the right. The left fist rests near the hip joint of the left leg; the right fist rests atop the right knee.

2. Grasp the handle of the sword with the right hand, the scabbard with the left, and rotate the sword outward slightly while moving the left knee inward.

3. Begin to rise onto the balls of both feet.

4. Continue to rise while drawing the sword straight ahead, level with the floor.

5. As soon as the sword tip clears the scabbard, step back with the left foot and drive downwards and sideways with the flat of the sword.

6. Move the left knee straight down until it rests on the floor. Begin to raise the sword overhead.

7. Bring the sword to the overhead position. Move the left hand up to grasp the handle. Slide the right foot slightly forward.

8. Cut straight down the center while pulling in with the right foot.

9–16. Perform chiburi and finish as in Kasumi (p. 190).

Three • Blocked at the Door

Sanbon Me • Tozume

戸
詰

Scenario. A swordsman sits in a doorway, facing two opponents, one on the left and one on the right. As the opponent on the left begins to attack, the swordsman draws and cuts that opponent across the wrists, then turns and finishes his other opponent with a downward cut, flips the blood off his sword and resheathes it, before standing up with dignity.

1. Sit facing directly toward the shomen, left left tucked under the body and right foot tucked near the left knee. The right knee should be up, so that the leg makes a 45° angle upward toward the right. The left fist rests near the hip joint of the left leg; the right fist rests atop the right knee.

2. Grasp the handle of the sword with the right hand, the scabbard with the left, and rotate the sword outward slightly while moving the left knee inward.

195

3. Begin to rise onto the balls of the feet while drawing the sword upward and toward the right front corner.

4. Step out to the right front corner with the right leg. As soon as the tip of the sword clears the scabbard, flip the sword in a diagonal path toward the right front. Extend out with the arm. The sword tip should stop at shoulder height. Pull the scabbard back with the left hand.

5. Adjust the body to face the left front by stepping to the left with the right foot. Raise the sword to the overhead position. Move the left hand up to grasp the handle.

6. Cut straight down center while pulling in with the right foot.

7–14. Perform chiburi and finish as in Kasumi (p. 190), stepping with the left foot first to adjust the body to face straight ahead.

Four • Beneath the Doorway

Yonhon Me • Towaki

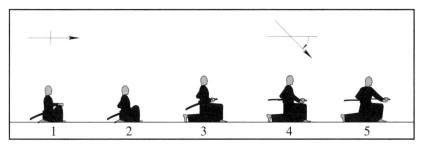

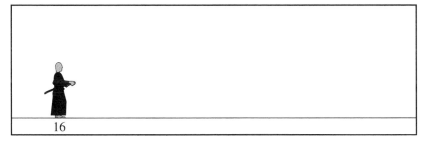

Scenario. A swordsman sits in a doorway. Two opponents, one on the left rear and one on the right front, prepare to attack. As the opponent in the rear begins to attack, the swordsman draws and thrusts his sword into that opponent, then turns and finishes his other opponent with a downward cut. Finally, he flips the blood off his sword and resheathes it before standing up with dignity.

1. Sit facing the shomen, left left tucked under the body and right foot tucked near the left knee. The right knee should be up, so that the leg makes a 45° angle upward toward the right. The left fist rests near the hip joint of the left leg; the right fist rests atop the right knee.

2. Grasp the handle of the sword with the right hand, the scabbard with the left, and rotate the sword outward slightly while moving the left knee inward.

3. Step out toward the right front corner with the right leg.

4. Begin to draw the sword, level with the floor, toward the right front. Rotate the blade outward while drawing until it is flat side up.

5. Continue drawing until the tip clears the scabbard.

6. As soon as the tip clears the scabbard, look toward the left rear, pull the scabbard back with the left hand, and thrust toward the left rear corner with the sword tip. The scabbard should be pulled back until it is perpendicular to the line of the sword. The sword should be stopped when the tsuba is in front of the left pectoral muscle.

7. Bring the sword to the overhead position. Move the left hand up to grasp the handle. Slide the right foot slightly forward.

8. Cut straight down the center while pulling in with the right foot.

9–16. Perform chiburi and finish as in Kasumi (p. 190).

Five • Four Directional Cut

Gohon Me • Shihogiri

四
方
切

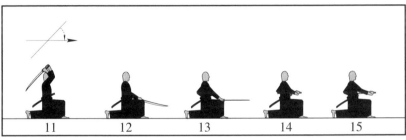

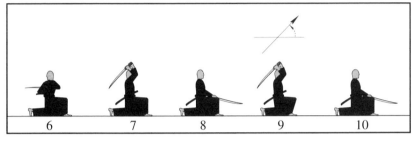

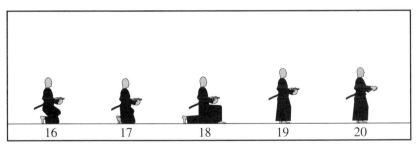

Scenario. A swordsman sits, surrounded by four opponents. Seizing an opening, the swordsman rises, draws, and thrusts his sword into the opponent at his left rear. He then turns and cuts the opponents at the right front, the left front, and at center. Finally, he flips the blood off his sword and resheathes it before standing up with dignity.

1. Sit facing the shomen, left left tucked under the body and right foot tucked near the left knee. The right knee should be up, so

that the leg makes a 45° angle upward toward the right. The left fist rests near the hip joint of the left leg; the right fist rests atop the right knee.

2. Grasp the handle of the sword with the right hand, the scabbard with the left, and rotate the sword outward slightly while moving the left knee inward.

3. Step out toward the right front corner with the right leg.

4. Begin to draw the sword, level with the floor, toward the right front. Rotate the blade outward while drawing until it is flat side up.

5. Continue drawing until the tip clears the scabbard.

6. As soon as the tip clears the scabbard, look toward the left rear, pull the scabbard back with the left hand, and thrust toward the left rear corner with the sword tip. The scabbard should be pulled back until it is perpendicular to the line of the sword. The sword should be stopped when the tsuba is in front of the left pectoral muscle.

7. Bring the sword to the overhead position. Move the left hand up to grasp the handle. Slide the right foot slightly forward.

8. Cut straight down the center while pulling in with the right foot.

9. Turn toward the left front corner by stepping across the front of the body with the right foot. At the same time, raise the sword overhead.

10. Cut straight down toward the left front corner.

11. Turn toward the left front corner by stepping across the front of the body with the right foot. At the same time, raise the sword overhead.

12. Cut straight down the center.

13–20. Perform chiburi and finish as in Kasumi (p. 190).

Six • Beneath the Ledge

Roppon Me • Tanashita

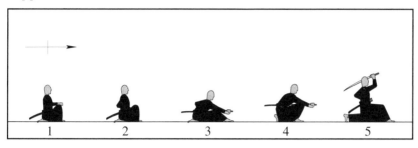

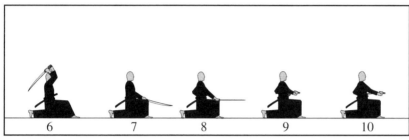

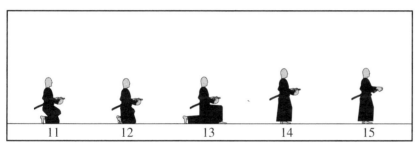

Scenario. A swordsman sits beneath a ledge, facing out toward an opponent. He slides forward to get out from under the ledge, where he is attacked by the opponent. The swordsman draws and raises his sword to parry the attack, then finishes the opponent with a downward cut. Finally, he flips the blood off his sword and resheathes it before standing up with dignity.

1. Sit facing the shomen, left left tucked under the body and right foot tucked near the left knee. The right knee should be up, so the leg makes a 45° angle upward toward the right. The left fist rests near the hip joint of the left leg; the right fist rests on the right knee.

2. Grasp the handle of the sword with the right hand, the scabbard with the left, and rotate the sword outward slightly while moving the left knee inward.

3. Slide the right foot straight ahead while dropping the head and drawing the sword straight ahead and level with the floor.

4. Pull the left leg forward. Continue drawing the sword, and when it clears the scabbard, begin to raise it, handle higher than the tip, butt forward. Pull the scabbard back with the left hand.

5. Rise into a kneeling position by sliding the right foot forward and straightening the body. Raise the sword to the overhead position.

6. Move the left hand up to grasp the handle.

7. Cut straight down the center.

8–15. Perform chiburi and finish as in Kasumi (p. 190).

Seven • Blocked on Both Sides

Nanahon Me • Ryozume

両
詰

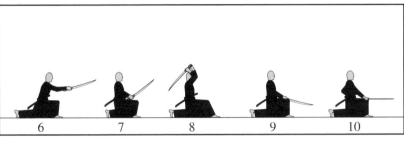

Scenario. A swordsman sits in a narrow corridor, facing an opponent. As the opponent prepares to attack, the swordsman flips his sword tip out to trap the opponent's wrists before he can draw. He then thrusts the sword into the opponent, slides forward and finishes the opponent with a downward cut. Finally, he flips the blood off his sword and resheathes it before standing up with dignity.

203

1. Sit facing the shomen, left left tucked under the body and right foot tucked near the left knee. The right knee should be up, so that the leg makes a 45° angle upward toward the right. The left fist rests near the hip joint of the left leg; the right fist rests atop the right knee.

2. Grasp the handle of the sword with the right hand, the scabbard with the left, and rotate the sword outward slightly while moving the left knee inward.

3. Rise into a kneeling position, without stepping out with the right leg, while drawing the sword upward, straight ahead. Pull the scabbard back with the left hand.

4. When the sword tip clears the scabbard, flip it to chudan position. Move the left hand to grasp the handle.

5. Slide the right foot forward.

6. Pull in with the right foot and drive forward with the tip of the sword.

7. Slide the left knee forward until it is even with the right foot. Return the sword to chudan position.

8. Raise the sword to the overhead position while sliding the right foot forward.

9. Cut straight down the center.

10–17. Perform chiburi and finish as in Kasumi (p. 190).

Eight • Charging the Tiger
Hachihon Me • Torabashiri

虎
走

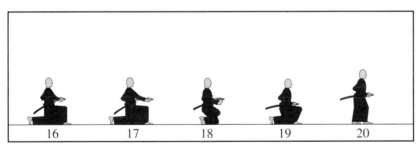

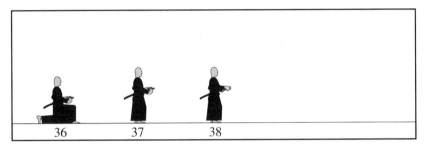

Scenario. A swordsman faces an opponent. Both are seated. They rise out of seiza, and the opponent begins to retreat. The swordsman draws to parry an attack by the opponent, then attacks with a downward strike. He flips the blood off the sword and replaces it in the scabbard, but the opponent prepares to attack again. The swordsman retreats as the opponent approaches, then draws his sword to parry the attack. He finishes the opponent with a downward cut, flips the blood off his sword, replaces it in the scabbard and stands up with dignity.

1. Sit facing directly toward the shomen, left left tucked under the body and right foot tucked near the left knee. The right knee should be up, so that the leg makes a 45° angle upward toward the right. The left fist rests near the hip joint of the left leg; the right fist rests atop the right knee.

2. Grasp the handle of the sword with the right hand, the scabbard with the left, and rotate the sword outward slightly while moving the left knee inward.

3. Begin to rise into a standing position. Slide the right foot slightly forward.

4. Stand, keeping the knees slightly bent and the center of gravity low.

5–8. Move forward four steps, left foot first, then right.

9. On the fifth step (left foot forward) begin to draw the sword straight ahead, toward throat level.

10. Step out with the right foot and cut horizontally across the front of the body, stopping the cut when the arm is 45° to the front right. The sword points straight ahead. Arm and sword are level. Pull the scabbard back with the left hand.

11. Move the left knee forward while dropping toward the floor. Begin to raise the sword.

12. Stop with the left knee even with the right foot. Raise the sword to the overhead position. Move the left hand up to grasp the handle.

13. Slide the right foot slightly forward.

14. Cut straight down the center. Pull in with the right foot and hips for power.

15. Perform chiburi by whipping the sword to the right at hip level. Move the left hand back to press against the scabbard.

16. Grasp the scabbard with the left hand, forming a cradle at the opening with the thumb and forefinger. Move the sword across the front of the body until it rests on the finger cradle at a point on the blade about six inches from the tsuba.

17. Slide the sword away from the body at a 45° angle until the tip reaches the opening of the scabbard. Keep it level.

18. Begin to slide the sword into the scabbard. Once the tip is inside the scabbard, move the first two-thirds of the blade into the scabbard in one quick motion. At the same time, slide the right foot back until it is even with the right.

19. Begin to rise by sliding the left foot back.

20. Stand, keeping the knees bent and the center of gravity low.

21–24. Move backward four steps, right foot first, then left.

25. On the fifth step (right foot back) begin to draw the sword straight ahead, toward throat level.

26. Step back with the left foot and cut horizontally across the front of the body. Pull the scabbard back with the left hand.

27. Move the left knee forward while dropping toward the floor. Begin to raise the sword.

28. Stop with the left knee even with the right foot. Raise the sword fully to the overhead position. Move the left hand up to grasp the sword handle.

29. Slide the right foot slightly forward.

30. Cut straight down the center. Pull in with the right foot and hips for power.

31–38. Perform chiburi and finish as in Kasumi (p. 190).

Secret Forms, Extra Set

The advanced techniques of the Extra Set (*Bangai no Bu*) were created to teach methods of dealing with larger numbers of opponents and with more sustained action. For the most part, they are combinations of standing forms from earlier sets, although the fourth form, *Shihogiri*, which shares its name with two other forms in this book, is completely new.

The length of these forms will expose any weaknesses in the student's balance, concentration, and control of the sword. Regular practice is the only means of overcoming these difficulties, and slow, methodical performance of each detail will yield the best progress. The names of the forms are as follows:

1. Fast Wave	*Hayanami*	210
2. Thunder and Lightning	*Raiden*	213
3. Thunderclap	*Jinrai*	216
4. Four Directional Cut (Demon Cutting)	*Shihogiri* (*Akumabarai*)	219

番外の部

速波

One • Fast Wave

Ippon Me • Hayanami

Scenario. A swordsman faces an array of opponents. He moves forward to engage an attacker at his right front, and flips his sword out to cut the attacker's wrists before an attack can come. He turns to the left front and cuts down an opponent there, then raises the sword overhead to parry an attack from another man at the front. Dropping his sword to abdomen level, he executes a 180° turn, cutting several nearby opponents in the process. He then finishes an opponent at the rear with a downward stroke, turns and finishes the last opponent in front, flips the blood off his sword and resheathes it with dignity.

1. Stand facing the shomen. Shoulders should be pulled back and down, hands held relaxed at the sides.

2. Step forward with the right foot. Let the left arm swing forward.

3. Step forward with the left foot, letting the right arm swing forward.

4. Step forward with the right foot while grasping the scabbard with the left hand.

5. Take a half step forward with the left foot. Grasp the handle of the sword with the right hand.

6. Begin to draw the sword, upward and toward the right front corner.

7. Take a large step toward the right front corner while cutting on a diagonal path in the same direction. Extend the sword tip. Pull the scabbard back with the left hand.

8. Move to face the left front corner by stepping across the front with the right foot. Raise the sword to the overhead position and move the left hand up to grasp the handle.

9. Cut straight down toward the left front corner.

10. Raise the sword horizontally to protect the head from a frontal attack. The tip should extend toward the right and the widest third of the blade should be directly above and in front of the head.

11. Bring the left foot forward to a position even with the right.

12. Lower the sword to a horizontal position at hip level on the left side of the body.

13. Step back and toward the left with the right foot.

14–16. Begin to cut in a horizontal arc passing to the right in front of the body. Pivot 180° to face the rear while continuing the cut and finish the motion by bringing the sword all the way up to the overhead position.

17. Cut straight down toward the rear.

18. Turn 180° to the left while raising the sword to the overhead position.

19. Cut straight down the center.

20–25. Perform chiburi and finish as in Yukizure (p. 157).

Two • Thunder and Lightning

Nihon • Raiden

雷
電

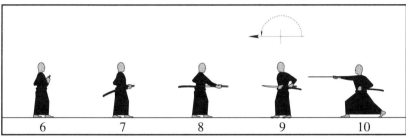

Scenario. A swordsman walks among several opponents. When an opponent grabs the butt of his scabbard, he forces the opponent off balance by suddenly pulling in on the sword. He draws, turns, and impales the opponent before finishing him with a downward cut. He then moves the sword to abdomen level, turns, cutting several opponents in the process, and finishes an opponent in the front with a downward stroke. Finally, he flips the blood off his sword and resheaths it with dignity.

1. Stand facing the shomen. Shoulders should be pulled back and down, hands held relaxed at the sides.

2. Step forward with the right foot. Let the left arm swing forward.

3. Step forward with the left foot, letting the right arm swing forward.

4. Step forward with the right foot while grasping the scabbard with the left hand.

5. Look back over the left shoulder while rotating the handle inward and downward with the left hand.

6. Step forward with the left foot while bringing the sword and scabbard up to the center in a circular motion.

7. Step forward with the right foot. Bring the sword and scabbard down and forward until they are nearly level.

8. Begin to draw the sword straight ahead, level with the floor. Pull the scabbard back with the left hand.

9. As soon as the tip of the sword clears the scabbard, pivot to face the front by turning to the left. Pivot on the right heel, then the left heel. Pull the scabbard fully back with the left hand and keep the sword close to the body with the right. The sword should be level and the right hand should be behind the hip.

10. Adjust the body to face fully forward by stepping slightly to the left with the left foot and back and slightly to the right with the right foot. Thrust forward with the tip of the sword.

11. Bring the sword back to chudan position and grasp the handle near the butt with the left hand.

12. Raise the sword to the overhead position while stepping forward with the right foot. The foot should be about one-half foot's length further back than the left.

13. Step out with the right foot and cut straight down.

14. Raise the sword tip straight up, bringing the tsuba up until it is even with the chin.

15. Lower the sword to the left side of the body so that it is level with the floor.

16–17. Cut on a horizontal path at hip level while pivoting toward the front. Continue the motion to bring the sword to the overhead position.

18. Shift forward on the right foot and cut straight down center.

19–24. Chiburi and finish as in Yukizure (p. 157).

迅
雷

Three · Thunderclap

Sanbon Me · Jinrai

Scenario. A swordsman walks among a group. Some of the members of the group are opponents, some are allies. Seizing an opening, he draws his sword and thrusts it into an opponent at his left rear, turns, and cuts down opponents at the right front, left front, and front center. Seeing another opponent ahead, he uses the flat of his sword to push his allies clear, and steps forward to cut down that opponent. Finally, he flips the blood off his sword and resheathes it with dignity.

1. Stand facing the shomen. Shoulders should be pulled back and down, hands held relaxed at the sides.

2. Step forward with the right foot. Let the left arm swing forward.

3. Step forward with the left foot, letting the right arm swing forward.

4. Step forward with the right foot while grasping the scabbard with the left hand.

5. Look back over the left shoulder while rotating the handle inward and downward with the left hand.

6. Step out toward front right while preparing to draw the sword on the same angle, parallel to the floor. Rotate the sword and scabbard outward until the blade is flat (parallel to the floor).

7. Draw the sword until only the tip remains inside the scabbard.

8. Look back toward the left rear corner. Pull the scabbard back with the left hand until it is perpendicular to the path made by the sword, clearing the sword tip. Thrust the sword back toward the left rear corner, stopping with the tsuba touching the left pectoral area.

9. Turn to face the right front corner and raise the sword overhead. Move the left hand up to grasp the handle.

10. Cut straight down toward the right front corner.

11. Step all the way forward to the left front corner with the right foot while raising the sword overhead.

12. Cut straight down toward the left front corner.

13. Step directly toward the front with the right foot while raising the sword overhead.

14. Cut straight down the center.

15. Bring the right foot back, even with the left, and move the sword hand back so that the hands cross at the wrists. The sword should rest on the sleeve of the left arm, at a point midway between the shoulder and elbow. Slide the right thumb back to press against the side of the handle to keep the sword blade flat (straight up and down) for the next two motions.

16. Rise onto the ball of the left foot, lift the right foot off the ground, and raise the wrists up to the level of the top of the head.

17. Simultaneously drop and slide the right foot forward while expanding outward with both hands. The sword should move on a horizontal path until it points directly out to the right.

18. Step forward with the left foot and continue the motion of both hands until the sword reaches the overhead position. Grasp the handle with the left hand.

19. Step forward with the right foot, then cut straight down center.

20–25. Perform chiburi and finish as in Yukizure (p. 157).

Four • Four Directional Cut (Demon Cutting)

Yonhon Me • Shihogiri (Akumabarai)

四方切・悪魔払

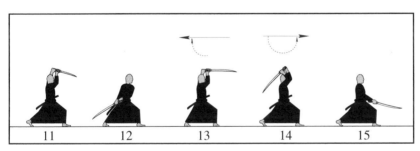

Scenario. A swordsman walks into a group of four opponents. At a crucial moment, he turns to the right, draws his sword and thrusts it into the opponent at the left side, then faces the right and strikes the opponent there on the forehead. That opponent strikes and the swordsman parries the strike, then makes a sweeping cut across the front and side, striking both the opponent on the right and in the rear. He then cuts the rear opponent with a rising cut and turns to cut down the opponent in the front with a downward stroke. Finally, he flips the blood off his sword and resheathes it with dignity.

1. Stand facing the shomen. Shoulders should be pulled back and down, hands held relaxed at the sides.

2. Step forward with the right foot. Let the left arm swing forward.

3. Step forward with the left foot, letting the right arm swing forward.

4. Step forward with the right foot while grasping the scabbard with the left hand.

5. Step forward with the left foot. Grasp the handle with the right hand.

6. Step out toward the right side with the right foot. The sword and scabbard should be held level with the ground. Prepare to draw the sword directly toward the right side.

7. Draw the sword, keeping it level with the floor. The blade angle should be flat.

8. As soon as the sword clears the scabbard, thrust back toward the left side. Stop with the tsuba even with the left pectoral muscle.

9. Turn to face the right side while raising the sword to the overhead position.

10. Strike toward forehead level.

11. Move the hands up on the left side to bring the sword to a guard position in front of the head, tip pointing toward the rear (the body's right side).

12. In one motion, bring the left foot slightly forward, then step fully back with the right and sweep all the way across the front of the body with the sword. Continue the motion until the sword is pointing back and downward, hands near the right hip.

13. Without stopping, step toward the rear with the right foot while cutting in an upward arc toward the rear (the body's front), stopping when the sword is above the head, level with the floor.

14. Pivot 180° to face the front.

15. Cut directly down the center.

16–21. Perform chiburi and finish as in Yukizure (p. 157).

Sword Methods

刀
法

The techniques of Sword Methods (*Toho*) were selected by the All Japan Iaido Federation as a representative set of forms from the various traditional styles of swordsmanship. Each form has a unique character that shows something of the nature of the style in which it originated. The difficulty of the forms is generally thought to increase from number 1 to 5, although all but the first will present a challenge to the student of Eishin-Ryu, since there are several unaccustomed movements in each. There is also the audible kiai, which is not normally used in Eishin-Ryu practice, and which makes the cut more difficult at first. Sincere practice over a period of several years will solve this difficulty, however, and eventually give far more power to the cut. The names of the forms and their parent systems are as follows:

1. Forward Cut   *Maegiri (Eishin-Ryu)*   223
2. Forward and Rearward Cut   *Zengogiri (Mugai-Ryu)*   226
3. Rising Cut   *Kiriage (Shindo Munen-Ryu)*   229
4. Four Directional Cut   *Shihogiri (Suio-Ryu)*   232
5. Tip Flip   *Kissaki Gaeshi (Hoki-Ryu)*   235

One • Forward Cut

Ippon Me • Maegiri

前
切

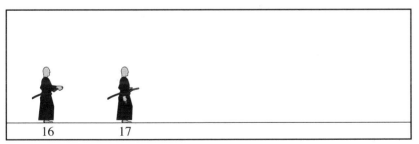

Scenario. A swordsman faces an opponent. Both are seated. As the opponent prepares to attack, the swordsman quickly draws and cuts him across the throat, then finishes him with a downward cut. Flipping the blade to remove any blood, the swordsman resheathes his sword and stands up in a dignified manner.

1. Sit in seiza, facing forward, with the back straight, chin tucked, and hands flat on the thighs with fingers together.

223

2. Grasp the scabbard with the left hand. Grasp the handle of the sword, near the tsuba, with the right hand. Rotate the edge of the sword outward about 30° while moving the knees together.

3. Begin to draw the sword directly ahead and toward throat level while rising onto the knees. Rise onto the balls of the feet. Use the left hand to pull the scabbard back toward the obi. Rotate the edge of the sword to 90° (flat) just before movement 5.

4. Draw the sword on a horizontal line in front of the body. Simultaneously step out with the right leg. The finished position should be as follows: shoulders square; right arm extending toward the right front corner, level with the floor. The blade should be level, pointing straight ahead.

5. Bring the sword overhead, keeping the tip lower than the handle throughout the motion.

6. Move the left hand up to grasp the handle.

7. Cut down center. Stop the sword so that the butt of the handle is one fist length from the abdomen.

8. Perform chiburi by whipping the sword to the side at hip level. The right hand should be forward of the body, the sword level and pointing straight ahead.

9. Move the sword across the front of the body until it rests on the finger cradle at a point on the blade about six inches from the tsuba. The sword should be level, its edge at about a 60° angle below straight up and down.

10. Slide the sword away from the body at a 45° angle until the tip reaches the opening of the scabbard. Keep it level.

11. Begin to slide the sword into the scabbard. Slide the right foot straight back at the same time, so that comes even with the left foot just as the sword seats in the scabbard.

12. Let the left hand slide back when it is contacted by the scabbard. As soon as the sword is fully seated, place the thumb of the left hand on the tsuba.

13. Move the right hand to the butt of the handle. Grasp the handle at that point.

14. Step out with the right foot.

15. Stand up by stepping back with the right foot.

16. Adjust the sword back to its centered position.

17. Move the right hand down to a relaxed position at the side of the body. Step back to the starting position, left foot first.

Two • Forward and Rearward Cut

Nihon Me • Zengogiri

前後切

Scenario. A swordsman is seated between two opponents, also seated, one facing him from the back, one from the front. As the opponent in front prepares to attack, the swordsman quickly draws, blocking the attack, and strikes at his forehead, then turns and finishes the opponent in the rear with a downward cut. He then turns back to the front and finishes the first opponent with a downward cut. Flipping the blade to remove any blood, the swordsman resheathes his sword and stands up in a dignified manner.

1. Sit in seiza, facing forward, with the back straight, chin tucked, hands flat on the thighs just above midway up from the knees with the fingers together.

2. Grasp the scabbard with the left hand.   Grasp the handle of the sword, near the tsuba, with the right hand.

3. Begin to draw the sword upward while rising onto the knees. Rise onto the balls of the feet. Use the left hand to pull the scabbard back toward the obi.

4. As soon as the sword clears the scabbard, draw it so that it intersects the centerline, then raise it to the overhead position, with the tip above the handle. Move the left hand up to grasp the handle.

5. Strike directly forward at forehead level.

6. Turn 180° to the left, while raising the sword to the overhead position, by rising into a standing position and pivoting on the heels.

7. Cut down the center toward the rear while dropping gently onto the right knee. Stop the sword so that the butt of the handle is one fist length from the abdomen.

8. Turn 180° to the right, while raising the sword to the overhead position, by rising into a standing position and pivoting on the heels.

9. Cut down the center toward the front while dropping gently onto the left knee.

10. Raise the tip of the sword to throat level by lifting with the right hand.

11. Perform chiburi by whipping the sword to the side at hip level. The right hand should be forward of the body, the sword level and pointing straight ahead.

12. Move the sword across the front of the body until it rests on the finger cradle at a point on the blade about six inches from the tsuba.

The sword should be level, its edge at about a 60° angle below straight up and down.

13. Slide the sword away from the body at a 45° angle until the tip reaches the opening of the scabbard. Keep it level.

14. Begin to slide the sword into the scabbard. Slide the right foot straight back at the same time, so that comes even with the left foot just as the sword seats in the scabbard.

15. Let the left hand slide back when it is contacted by the scabbard. As soon as the sword is fully seated, place the thumb of the left hand on the tsuba.

16. Move the right hand to the butt of the handle. Grasp the handle at that point.

17. Step out with the right foot.

18. Stand up by stepping back with the right foot.

19. Adjust the sword back to its centered position.

20. Move the right hand down to a relaxed position at the side of the body. Step back to the starting position, left foot first.

Three • Rising Cut

Sanbon Me • Kiriage

切上

Scenario. A swordsman stands, facing an opponent. As the opponent prepares to attack, the swordsman moves forward and draws his sword in a rising motion to cut the opponent. He then finishes him with a downward cut. Flipping the blade to remove any blood, the swordsman resheathes his sword and stands up in a dignified manner.

1. Stand facing the shomen. Shoulders should be pulled back and down, hands held relaxed at the sides.

229

2. Grasp the scabbard with the left hand.

3. Step forward with the right foot.

4. Grasp the handle of the sword with the right hand.

5. Step forward with the left foot. Begin to draw the sword, keeping it level with the floor. When the sword is two-thirds out of the scabbard, rotate both sword and scabbard outward until the sword edge is facing down.

6. Take a large step forward with the right foot while continuing to draw the sword. Draw the sword on a rising angle across the front of the body, from the lower left side moving toward the upper right. At the end of the cut, the sword should be above and to the right of the head, parallel to the floor, pointing straight ahead with the edge up. The left heel is down.

7. Move the left foot forward, to within one foot of the right, while raising the sword overhead. Move the left hand up to the handle.

8. Cut on the kesa angle (upper right to lower left) while stepping out with the right foot. The body should turn slightly so that the right hip and shoulder end up forward of the left. Left heel is down.

9. Turn the body to face straight ahead while raising the sword to chudan position. The left heel comes up off the ground.

10. Perform chiburi by whipping the sword to the side at hip level. The right hand should be forward of the body, the sword level and pointing straight ahead. Move the left hand back to press against the scabbard.

11. Grasp the scabbard with the left hand, forming a cradle at the opening with the thumb and forefinger. Move the sword across the front of the body until it rests on the finger cradle at a point on the blade about six inches from the tsuba. The sword should be level, its edge at about a $60°$ angle below straight up and down.

12. Slide the sword away from the body at a $45°$ angle until the tip reaches the opening of the scabbard. Keep it level.

13. Slide the sword into the scabbard slowly. Let the left hand slide back when it is contacted by the scabbard. As soon as the sword is fully seated, place the thumb of the left hand on the tsuba.

14. Move the right hand to the butt of the handle. Grasp the handle at that point.

15. Slide the left foot forward to bring it even with the right. Adjust the sword back to its original position at the center of the body.

16. Move the right hand down to a relaxed position at the side of the body. Step back to the starting position, left foot first.

四方切

Four • Four Directional Cut

Yonhon Me • Shihogiri

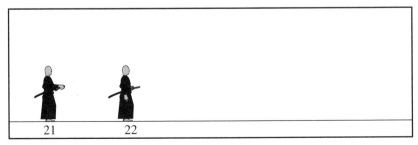

Scenario. A swordsman stands, surrounded by four opponents. As the opponent on his right prepares to attack, the swordsman steps out and cuts him on the wrist. He then turns and finishes the opponent on the right with a downward cut, turns and cuts several opponents across the middle with a horizontal cut, finishes the opponent in the rear, and turns and finishes the opponent in the front. Flipping the blade to remove any blood, he resheathes his sword and stands up in a dignified manner.

1. Stand facing the shomen. Shoulders should be pulled back and down, hands held relaxed at the sides.

2. Grasp the scabbard with the left hand.

3. Step forward with the right foot.

4. Step forward with the left foot, placing the foot in front of the right so that the toes point to the right. Grasp the handle of the sword with the right hand.

5. Look to the right. Begin to draw the sword on an upward angle.

6. Step out to the right and cut on an angle directly toward the right, stopping at wrist height.

7. Turn to face the left, bring the right foot even with the left, and raise the sword to the overhead position.

8. Step out to the left with the right foot while cutting straight down.

9. Raise the sword tip straight up until the tsuba is even with the chin.

10. Lower the sword to the left side of the body. It should be level and at hip height.

11. Step out toward the front with the right foot. Cut in a horizontal arc at hip level, bringing the sword 45° past straight ahead.

12. Turn 180° to the left while raising the sword to the overhead position.

13. Cut straight down toward the rear.

14. Turn 180° to the right while raising the sword to the overhead position.

15. Cut straight down the center.

16–22. Perform chiburi and finish as in Kiriage (p. 229).

Five • Tip Flip

Gohon Me • Kissaki Gaeshi

切
先
返

Scenario. A swordsman stands facing an opponent. As the opponent prepares to attack, the swordsman steps forward and draws his sword to parry the cut. He then twists his body suddenly, bringing the tip of his sword down to cut his opponent, thrusts forward into his belly, then finishes him with a downward cut. Flipping the blade to remove any blood, he resheathes his sword and stands up in a dignified manner.

1. Stand facing the shomen. Shoulders should be pulled back and down, hands held relaxed at the sides.

2. Grasp the scabbard with the left hand.

3. Step forward with the right foot.

4. Step forward with the left foot. Grasp the handle of the sword with the right hand.

5. Begin to draw the sword in an upward direction toward the right front corner.

6. Lift the sword to a position above and in front of the head, so that the blade is protecting the head in front and the tip points to the left. Bring the left hand up to support the blade. Place the hand at a point about one-third of the sword's length from the tip. The blade should rest on the pad of skin between the thumb and forefinger.

7. Adjust the blade to point directly backwards by moving the right hand forward and the left hand back. The butt should point directly ahead.

8. Turn the hips to the right to twist the body, so that the left knee touches the back of the right knee, while moving the sword in a downward arc in front of the body. The sword should travel along the centerline of the body.

9. Step forward with the left foot while thrusting straight ahead with the sword. The sword should stop when the tsuba is even with the hip. The fingers and thumb of the left hand should come together and the hand should press lightly, in a flat position, against the top of the blade.

10. Step all the way back with the left foot so that the right foot is forward, simultaneously executing the chiburi to the side.

11–16. Replace the sword in the scabbard and finish as in Kiriage (p. 229).

Glossary

AIKIDO (eye-KEY-dough): A defensive martial art synthesized from earlier forms by Ueshiba Morihei. Aikido includes various throwing and joint-locking methods and incorporates a strong philosophical outlook.

BANGAI NO BU (BON-guy-no-boo): Meaning extra, or un-numbered set, a set of four advanced forms in the Eishin-Ryu system.

BATTO HO NO BU (baht-TOE-hoe-no-boo): A set of eleven forms in the Eishin-Ryu system. The first seven forms are considered basic forms, the last four OKU NO WAZA, or secret techniques, taught at the intermediate level.

BATTO-JUTSU (baht-TOE-jutsu): A sword-drawing art similar to iaido. Most schools practice cutting rolled straw targets as well as solo and two-person forms.

BOSHI (BOW-she): Part of the Japanese sword. The small part of the JI above the YOKOTE.

BU (boo): A unit in the classical Japanese measuring system used to describe the length of swords, equal to approximately one centimeter.

BUDO (BU-dough): Martial arts. Literally means "the way of the warrior," connoting a lifetime of devotion to the principles and practices of a classical warrior.

CHIBURI (chee-BOO-ri): "Blood tossing." Flipping the blood off the sword after cutting an opponent. There are three major methods in Eishin-Ryu.

CHOKUTO (CHOKE-toe): Straight sword commonly used in early historical Japan.

DAISHO (DIE-show): Literally "big small," refers to the set of two swords carried by full-ranking samurai. One was larger, the KATANA, and the other smaller, called the *wakizashi*.

EDO PERIOD (EH-dough): 1600–1867. Japan was ruled during this time by the Tokugawa military government. Because a lasting peace was established during this period, swordsmanship became more of an art form and less a fighting method.

FUKURA (FOO-coo-rah): The curve of the tip of the sword above the YOKOTE.

FURIKABURI (foo-ri-KAH-BOO-ri): To "hang" or "suspend." In iaido, refers to the lifting of the sword over one's head.

HA (hah): The sharp edge of the sword blade.

HABAKI (hah-BAH-key): The short metal sleeve near the handle of the sword.

HAKAMA (hah-KAH-ma): The divided skirt worn by Japanese martial artists.

HAMACHI (HAH-MA-chee): Notch at the edge of a sword blade, separating the cutting edge from the tang.

HAMON (HAH-moan): The temper line on the sides of the sword.

HEIAN PERIOD (HEY-on): 782–1184. Japan's capital was located in Kyoto during this period, which saw the evolution of the TACHI.

HOKI-RYU (ho-KEY-ryou): A style of iaido founded by Katayama Hokinokami Hisayasu and recognized by the All Japan Iaido Federation.

JI (gee): The flat surface of the sword blade.

JO, HA, KYU (joe, hah, cue): The three parts of NUKITSUKE (drawing the sword), which are "preparation, drawing, and sudden cut." The draw is supposed to begin slowly, gradually speed up, and move very quickly near the end.

JUDO (JU-dough): The "way of flexibility," judo was created as a method of physical development by Kano Jigoro, and includes throwing and pinning techniques. It is now practiced as a competitive sport around the world.

KAESU (kais): To flip, or return. In iaido, refers to any motion in which the sword's position is reversed suddenly.

KAMAKURA PERIOD (KAH-MAH-coo-rah): 1185–1332. The seat of the military government was in Kamakura during this period. Considered the golden age of the Japanese sword, when some of the finest examples of TACHI were produced.

KARATEDO (kah-RAH-TEH-dough): The "way of the empty hand." An art form for character development and self-defense which includes punching, kicking, blocking and stepping motions. Karate originated in Okinawa, a synthesis of local and Chinese fighting methods, and later became popular in central Japan.

KATANA (kah-TAH-NAH): The modern Japanese sword. The blade is usually about ninety centimeters (thirty five inches) in length, slightly curved, and worn with the edge upwards, often in combination with the *wakizashi*.

KATANA-BUKURO (kah-TAH-NAH BOO-COO-row): A cover for the sword, usually made of cloth.

KATORI SHINTO-RYU (kah-TOE-REE SHIN-TOE ryou): The oldest extant martial art style in Japan. This art includes empty hand techniques as well as sword and other weapons skills.

KEN: Sword. Used specifically to refer to an ancient, two-edge sword made before the ninth century.

KENDO (KEN-dough): The "way of the sword." In modern times, refers to a sport practiced widely in Japan, in which the competitors wear light armor and strike designated target areas with a *shinai* (bamboo, swordlike weapon). Before the sport was created, KENDO referred to the art of the swordsman, who used real swords or wooden swords (BOKUTO).

KENJUTSU (KEN-jutsu): The "art of the sword," refers to various methods of sword fighting, but does not include the connotation of a philosophical component that kendo includes.

KIRIOROSHI (key-ree-oh-ROW-SHE): The downward cutting motion in iaido.

KISSAKI (KISS-saki): The tip of the sword.

KOIGUCHI (KOH-EE-guchi): The opening of the SAYA.

KOJIRI (koh-GEE-ree): The butt of the scabbard.

KOKUSAI BUDOIN (coke-SAI BOO-DOUGH-in): International Martial Arts Federation. This organization has branches in many countries around the world and promotes traditional Japanese martial arts. IMAF has both iaido and BATTO-JUTSU divisions.

KOSHINOGI (koh-she-NO-gi): The taper line of the sword above the YOKOTE.

KOTO (KOH-toe): Literally "old sword." Any sword made before the EDO PERIOD.

KURIGATA (coo-ree-GAH-tah): The wooden eyelet on the scabbard through which the SAGEO (cord) is threaded.

KYUDO (CUE-dough): Japanese archery. Like iaido, kyudo has no practical self-defense applications, so it is practiced primarily for its character development aspects. Strongly influenced by Zen.

MEI (may): A sword's name.

MEKUGI (meh-COO-gi): The wooden peg that secures the handle to the tang of the sword.

MEKUGI ANA (meh-COO-gi anna): The hole through the tang for the peg.

MENUKI (meh-NEW-key): Metal ornament placed inside the wrappings on the handle, to enhance the grip.

MONOUCHI (MOW-NO-uchi): The back of the blade at the top third near the tip.

MONTSUKI (MOHN-tski): Kimono top worn by Japanese at formal occasions. The *mon* is the family crest, usually a circular design, printed on the garment.

MOMOYAMA PERIOD (moh-MOH-YAH-ma): 1573–1599. The period in which samurai began to wear the DAISHO (pair of swords), and the beginning of the SHINTO (new sword) period.

MUGAI-RYU (moo-GUY-ryou): a style of iaido founded by Tsuji Mugai Gettan, and recognized by the All Japan Iaido Federation.

MUNE (MOO-neh): The back of a KATANA.

MUNEMACHI (MOO-NEH-MA-chee): The notch at the back of the sword that separates the blade from the tang.

MUROMACHI PERIOD (MOO-ROW-MA-chee): 1392–1572. A period of constant civil wars in which swords were manufactured in large numbers. The KATANA came to be used much more commonly than the TACHI during this period.

MUSO JIKIDEN EISHIN-RYU (moo-SEW GEE-KEY-den AY-SHIN ryou): The full name of the style of iaido that is the subject of this book. The name means "Peerless, Directly Transmitted True-Faith Style." Eishin-Ryu techniques descend directly from the iaido forms created and systematized by Hayashizaki Jinsuke Minamoto Shigenobu.

MUSO SHINDEN-RYU (moo-SEW SHIN-den ryou): The name of the overall system of iaido created by Hayashizaki Jinsuke Minamoto Shigenobu. Muso Shinden Ryu and Eishin Ryu split after eleven generations of leaders and are now practiced as distinct styles (see page 13 for a more complete explanation of the relationship between these two styles).

NAGASU (nah-GAH-sue): The verb "to flow" in Japanese, part of the compound *ukenagashi* to mean "parrying," the name of two techniques in the Eishin-Ryu system.

NAGINATA (nah-GI-NAH-tah): An old Japanese weapon composed of a long pole with a curved blade on one end.

NAGINATADO (nah-GI-NAH-tah dough): "The way of the naginata," a traditional Japanese martial art practiced with mock weapons (the blade is replaced with a split bamboo striking tool resembling the *shinai* used in KENDO). Naginatado is usually, but not exclusively, practiced by women in Japan. Competitions take place with the competitors wearing light body armor and scoring points by striking designated spots on their opponent's bodies.

NAKAGO (NAH-KAH-go): The tang of the sword.

NAMBOKUCHO PERIOD (nahm-BOK-cho): 1333–1391. The NAGINATA was widely used as a weapon during this period, in which there were two rival lines of emperors vying for power.

NOTO (NOH-toe): To "replace the sword," the last motion with the sword in most iaido forms.

NOBASU (noh-BAS): To "extend," a commonly used instruction in iaido practice. Students are often told to "extend with the sword," or to extend their arms or legs.

NUKITSUKE (new-KEY-tskay): The correct name for the draw. Nukitsuke applies to the entire drawing motion, from the first movement of the sword to the first stopping point at the end of the motion.

OBI (OH-be): "Belt," the obi used in iaido, a wide, stiff piece of cloth long enough to wrap around the body three or more times.

OKUIAI (oh-coo-EH-AH-i): "Secret *iai*," secret techniques, originally kept hidden from anybody outside the system for strategic reasons, now taught only to intermediate and advanced students of the art.

OKUIAI: IWAZA NO BU (ee-WAH-zah no boo): "Secret Iaido: Seated Set," techniques performed from TATEHIZA, the seated position with one knee up.

OKUIAI: TACHIWAZA NO BU (tah-chee-WAH-zah no boo): "Secret Iaido: Standing Set."

OKU NO WAZA (OH-coo no wah-zah): "Secret Technique." Any secret technique from a Japanese art, such as OKUIAI from iaido.

SAGARU (sah-GAH-rue): To "step back," a command given at the end of an iaido form, when the student takes several steps back to his starting position.

SAGEO (sah-GAY-oh): The cord that attaches to the scabbard, used to prevent it from slipping out of the obi during practice.

SAGERU (sah-GEH-rue): To "lower," an instruction often heard during iaido practice. Students are often told to lower the sword, or lower their hips.

SAYA (SAH-yah): "Scabbard."

SEIZA (SAY-zah): "Correct sitting," the common seated posture in Japan. "Sitting on one's heels."

SEIZA NO BU (SAY-zah no boo): "Seated Set," the most basic set of techniques in Eishin-Ryu.

SEKIGUCHI-RYU (seh-KEY-GOO-chee ryou): A style of iaido founded by Sekiguchi Hachiroemon Ujishin and recognized by the All Japan Iaido Federation.

SEPPA (SEP-pah): A spacer, inserted between the HABAKI and the TSUBA on the KATANA.

SHAKU (shock): An archaic unit of measurement in Japan, used to refer to the length of swords. Equal to approximately one foot.

SHINDO MUNEN-RYU (SHIN-dough moo-NEN ryou): A style of iaido recognized by the All Japan Iaido Federation.

SHINOGI (she-NO-gi): The line on the blade of the sword that divides the two tapering flat surfaces of the blade.

SHINOGI JI (she-NO-gi gee): the flat surface of the blade above the shinogi.

SHIN SHINTO (shin SHIN-toe): "New new sword," any Japanese sword made after the Meiji Restoration (c. 1870).

SHINTO (SHIN-toe): "New sword," any sword made between about 1596 and the Meiji Restoration.

SHITAGI (SHTAH-gi): "Underwear," here a particular type of undergarment worn underneath the MONTSUKI for iaido practice.

SHU, HA, RI (shoe, hah, ri): Three stages of development in Japanese traditional learning. *Shu* is the stage at which you follow your instructor's teachings and, without changing them, practice obediently as you are told. *Ha* is the stage at which you try to improve your school by introducing some good points of the other schools. *Ri* is the stage at which you found a new school of your own. The All Japan Iaido Federation, which exists mainly to preserve traditional arts, purports that there are no *ha* or *ri* stages in its iaido.

SUIO-RYU (sue-ee-OH ryou): A style of iaido founded by Mima Yoichirozaemon Kagenobu and recognized by the All Japan Iaido Federation,

SUN (suhn): An archaic unit of measurement in Japan which is used to refer to the length of swords, equal to approximately one inch.

SUWARIWAZA (sue-WAH-RI-wah-zah): "Seated technique," any technique that originates from a seated position.

TABI (TAH-be): Split-toed socks worn in Japan. Many martial artists, including iaidoka and kyudoka, wear *tabi*.

TACHI (TAH-chee): A long, deeply curved sword used by mounted warriors in historical Japan.

TACHIWAZA (tah-CHEE WAH-zah): "Standing technique."

TAMIYA-RYU (tah-ME-AH ryou): A style of iaido founded by Tamiya Heibei Narimasa and recognized by the All Japan Iaido Federation.

TATEHIZA (tah-teh-HEE-zah): A half-seated position, similar to SEIZA but with the right knee raised. Commonly used by Japanese warriors because it allowed for quick movement into a position for defense or attack.

TATEHIZA NO BU (tah-teh-HEE-zah no bu): "Half-Seated Set," a set of techniques in iaido that begin in the TATEHIZA position.

TOHO NO BU (TOE-hoe no bu): "Sword Methods Set," a set of techniques compiled by the All Japan Iaido Federation. There are five techniques in this set, each selected from one of the iaido styles recognized by the federation.

TOYU, OTOYU (oh-TOE-you): Sword oil.

TSUBA (TSU-bah): The handguard on the Japanese sword.

TSUKA (tska): The handle of the Japanese sword.

TSUKAGASHIRA (tska-GAH-she-rah): The butt of the sword handle.

TSUKAITO (tska-EE-toe): The cord that wraps around the handle of the sword.

UCHIGATANA (ooh-CHEE-GA-TAH-nah): "Inside sword," one of the terms referring to the longer of two swords worn by the samurai.

UKERU (ooh-KEH-ru): To "receive," a term that includes any technique involving parrying an opponent's sword. Makes up part of the compound name of two iaido techniques called *ukenagashi*.

YOKOTE (yoh-COH-teh): A line on the sword at the beginning of the taper toward the tip.

ZEN NIHON IAIDO RENMEI: The All Japan Iaido Federation.

ZEN NIHON EISHIN-RYU IAIDO SEITO KAI: The All Japan Eishin-Ryu Traditions Association.

Bibliography

Craig, D. *Iai: The Art of Drawing the Sword*. Tokyo: Lotus Press, 1984.

Fukui, T. *Muso Jikiden Eishin-Ryu Iaido (Vols. 1 and 2)*. Gifu, Japan: Sugie Bijutsu Insatsu, 1978.

Kapp, L., Kapp, H. and Yoshihara, Y. *The Craft of the Japanese Sword*. Tokyo: Kodansha International, 1987.

Mitani, G. *Bunkai Iai: Muso Jikiden Eishin-Ryu* (Analysis of Iaido Techniques: Eishin-Style). Tokyo: Ski Journal Books, 1986.

Ogasawara, S. *Token* (Swords). Osaka: Hoikusha, 1985.

Ono, M. *Nihon Toh Shokunin Shokudan* (Japanese Sword Makers Discuss Their Craft). Tokyo: Komei Shuppan, 1973.

Ota, T. *Dosa Eishin-Ryu* (Eishin-Style Basics). Tokyo: Pelican, 1980.

Sasamori, J. and Warner, G. *This is Kendo*. Tokyo: Charles Tuttle, 1964.

Sato, K. *The Japanese Sword*. Tokyo: Kodansha International and Shibundo, 1983.

Warner, G. and Draeger, D.F. *Japanese Swordsmanship*. New York: Weatherhill, 1982.

Yamamoto, T. *Hagakure: The Book of the Samurai*. Translated by W.S. Wilson. Tokyo: Kodansha International, 1979.

Yamatsuta, R. *Muso Shinden-Ryu Iaido*. Tokyo: Airyudo.

Yumoto, J. *The Samurai Sword: A Handbook*. Tokyo: Charles Tuttle, 1958.

Index

Accompaniment, 157–158
Ai, vii
Aikido, 5, 8, 28
All Japan Iaido Federation, *vii*, 4, 13, 222
Amakuni, 8–9
Angular Sword, 93–94
Arai Seitetsu, 13
Arakawa Shozoemon, 13
Assisting at Seppuku, 65–67
Awareness, 29

Banno Denemon, 13
Batto Ho no Bu, 83–100, 114–125
Batto-Jutsu, 4, 8, 9
Beheading Stroke, 99–100
Beneath the Doorway, 197–198
Beneath the Ledge, 201–202
Between Walls, 175–176
Blade angle, 37, 41,104
Blocked at the Door, 195–196
Blocked on Both Sides, 203–204
Bokuto, 14
Boshi, 17
Bow, 27–35
Bowing to the *kamiza*, 30–31
Bowing to the sword, 28

Breaking Waves, 142–144
Budo, *vii*, *xi*, 10
Bushido, *x*, 11, 23, 24

Character, 103–104
Charging the Tiger, 205–208
Checkpoints, *ix*
Chiburi, 30
China, *x*, 8
Chokuto, 9
Cloud Bank, 127–129
Companions, 159–160
Complete Resolution, 161–163
Cutting, 39

Dignity, 109
Discipline, 23
Do, 10
Drawing, 37
Drawing Methods Set, 83–100, 114–125
Duty, *ix*, *x*

Eightfold Fences, 57–61
Eishin-Ryu Iaido, *ix*, *x*, 10, 13
Eishin-Ryu Iaido, Motto of 10
Encircled Leg, 193–194
Entering the Gate, 173–174
Excess motions, 103–104
Eye contact, 108

Face of the sword, 28
Facing Front, 154–155
Farewell Visit One, 179–180
Farewell Visit Three, 184–186
Farewell Visit Two, 181–183
Fast Wave, 210–212
Fish Scaling, 145–147
Flipping the blood off, 40
Floating Cloud, 136–138
Focus, 108
Forward, 44–46
Forward and Rearward Cut, 226–228
Forward Cut, 223–225
Forward Inverse Cut, 114–116
Four Directional Cut (Demon Cutting), 219–221
Four Directional Cut, 199–200, 232–234
Four Directional Cut One, 95–96
Four Directional Cut Two, 97–98
Fuchikane, 18
Fukui Harumasa, 13
Fukui Torao, 12, 13
Fukura, 17
Full Stop, 164–166
Fundamentals, 36–41
Furioroshi, 38

Gi, 14–15
Goto Masasuke, 13

Ha, 17
Hagakure, x
Hakama, 14–15, 20–22, 36, 106
Half-Seated Set, 126–155
Hamachi, 17
Hamon, 17
Hasegawa Mondonosuke, 13

Hayanami, 210–212
Hayashi Masu, 13
Hayashi Rokudayu, 13
Hayashi Yasudayu, 13
Hayashizaki Jinsuke, 12, 13
Hidari, 50–52
Hogiyama Namio, 13
Holding the sword, 39

I, vii
Iaidoka, 5, 6
Iaijutsu, 9–10
Iaito, 14
Inazuma, 133–135
Intermediate and advanced practice, 103–109
International Martial Arts Federation, 13
Itomagoi Sono Ichi, 179–180
Itomagoi Sono Ni, 181–183
Itomagoi Sono San, 184–186
Iwanami, 142–144

Ji, 17
Jinrai, 216–218
Judo, 5, 6, 8, 10
Jujutsu, 8, 10
Junto Sono Ichi, 84–86
Junto Sono Ni, 87–89
Jutsu, 10

Kabezoi, 175–176
Kaishaku, 65–67
Kamiza, 27, 30
Kanagawa Prefecture, 12
Karate, 5, 6, 8, 28
Kasumi, 190–192
Kata, 4
Katana, 9, 16
Kendo, 4, 8, 10
Kenjutsu, 3, 9, 10

Kenpo, 8
Kiai, 10, 108, 222
Kiriage, 229–231
Kirioroshi, 39
Kissaki, 17
Kissaki Gaeshi, 235–236
Koiguchi, 18
Kojiri, 18
Kokusai Budoin, IMAF, *viii*, 13
Kono Hyakuren, 12, 13
Korea, 8
Koshi, 38
Koshinogi, 17
Koteki Gyaku To, 120–122
Koteki Nukiuchi, 123–125
Kurigata, 18
Kyudo, 7, 11

Left, 50–52
Lightning, 133–135
Loyal Retainer, 167–168

Mae, 44–46
Maegiri, 223–225
Makkoh, 154–155
Martial Culture, *ix*
Mei, 17
Meiji Restoration, 9
Mekugi, 18
Mekugi Ana, 17
Menuki, 18
Metsuke, 108
Migi, 47–49
Misdirection, 169–170
Mist, 190–192
Momo Gumbei, 13
Moniri, 173–174
Monouchi, 17
Montsuki, 15, 21–22
Moonbeams, 72–75

Mountain Wind, 139–141
Moving, 36
Muga Mushin, 7
Multi-Directional Cut, 117–119
Mune, 17
Munemachi, 17
Muso Jikiden Eishin-Ryu Traditions Association, *vii*, 13
Muso Shinden-Ryu, 13

Nagano Muraku, 13
Nakago 17
Namigaeshi, 148–150
Noto, 41
Nukitsuke, 37
Nukiuchi, 80–82

Obi, 15, 20–22
Oe Masamichi, 13
Oikaze, 76–79
Oil, 14
Okuiai, Bangai no Bu, 209–221
Okuiai, Iwaza no Bu, 184–208
Okuiai, Tachiwaza no Bu, 156–186
Omote, 28
Ordered Sword One, 84–86
Ordered Sword Two, 87–89
Oroshi, 139–141
Oguro Motoemon, 13

Parrying (Seiza), 62–64
Parrying (Tachiwaza), 177–178
Pursuing Sword, 90–92
Pursuit, 68–71

Raiden, 213–215
Raising the sword, 38
Rear, 53–56
Rearward Inverse Cut, 120–122

Rearward Quick Draw, 123–125

Rei, 27–35

Reishiki, 11, 23

Returning the sword to the scabbard, 41

Returning Waves, 148–150

Right, 47–49

Rising Cut, 229–231

Ryozume, 203–204

Safety, 6

Sageo, 18

Samurai sitting method, 106–107

Saya, 18

Seated bow, 32–35

Seated Set, 43–82

Secret Forms, Seated Set, 184–208

Secret Forms, Standing Set, 156–186

Secret Techniques, Extra Set, 209–221

Seiza, 36

Seiza no Bu, 43–82

Sensei, 23

Seppa, 18

Shato, 93–94

Shihogiri (Akumabarai), 219–221

Shihogiri, 199–200, 232–234

Shihoto Sono Ichi, 95–96

Shihoto Sono Ni, 97–98

Shimmei Muso-Ryu, 12

Shinai, 4

Shinobu, 167–168

Shinogi, 17

Shinogi Ji, 17

Shinzen no rei, 30–31

Shomen, 27

Sitting, 36

Sleeve Flip, 171–172

Smithing, 8,16,19

So Dome, 164–166

So Makuri, 161–163

Sodesurigaeshi, 171–172

Soke, 12, 13

Speed of motions, 104

Standing, 36

Sudden Draw, 80–82

Sunegakoi, 193–194

Sword, 8,16, 22

Sword Methods, 222–236

Tabi, 15

Tachi, 9

Tailwind, 76–79

Takiotoshi, 151–153

Tamiya Heibei, 13

Tanashita, 201–202

Tanimura Kame, 13

Tatehiza, 106–107

Tatehiza no Bu, 126–155

Tateki To, 117–119

Thunder and Lightning, 213–215

Thunderclap, 216–218

Tiger's Step, 130–132

Tip Flip, 235–236

Toho, 222–236

Torabashiri, 205–208

Toraisoku, 130–132

Torei, 28

Towaki, 197–198

Tozume, 195–196

Tsuba, 18, 22

Tsuigeki To, 90–92

Tsuka, 18

Tsukagashira, 18

Tsukaito, 18

Tsukekomi, 68–71

Tsukikage, 72–75
Tsuredachi, 159–160

Ukenagashi, 62–64, 177–178
Ukigumo, 136–138
Urokogaeshi, 145–147
Ushiro, 53–56

Waterfall, 151–153
World War II, 10

Yaegaki, 57–61
Yamagata Prefecture, 12
Yamaguchi Katsuo, *vii*, *viii*, 3

Yamamoto Tsunenori, *x*
Yoda Manzo, 13
Yoga, 7
Yokogumo, 127–129
Yokote, 17
Yukichigai, 169–170
Yukizure, 157–158

Zanshin, 10, 109
Zantotosu To, 99–100
Zarei, 32–35
Zen, 7, 10
Zengo Giri, 226–228
Zenteki Gyaku To, 114–116

The "weathermark" identifies this book as a production of Weatherhill, Inc., publishers of fine books on Asia and the Pacific. Editorial supervision: Ray Furse. Book and cover design: Mariana Canelo Francis. Typography, illustrations, and page makeup: Nicklaus Suino. Production supervision: Bill Rose. Printing and binding: Command Web Offset, Secaucus, New Jersey.